Stepping on Memories

A Sister Remembers
The *Great* Depression and World War II

Marge Griffin-Glausier

firstWorks Publishing

Stepping On Memories

Published by FirstWorks Publishing Co., Inc.
www.firstworkspublishing.com
For Information, please address:
FirstWorks Publishing Co., Inc.
P.O. Box 93
Marietta, GA 30061-0093

Cover Design by Audra Pettyjohn, Graphic Artist
Evolution Designs, Dawsonville, GA

Ms. Glausier's Photo by Tiffany Studios
Ft. Lauderdale, FL

Agnes D'Alema's Photo by Guy D'Alema

Library of Congress Control Number 2004101440

ISBN: 0-9716158-4-5
ISBN: 978-0-9716158-4-7

Printed in the United States of America

All to Myself

All to myself I think
of you.
Think of the things
we used to do.
Think of the things
we used to say.
Think of each happy
yesterday.
Sometimes I sigh, and
sometimes I smile.
But I keep each olden,
golden while
All to myself.

From the Writings of
Wilbur D. Nesbit
--A. Buzza Motto / 1917--

Agnes Griffin-D'Alema

Personalities of The South - Tenth Edition
The World Who's Who of Women - Fifth Edition
Dictionary of International Biography - XVI Edition
The American Cultural s Registry - First Edition

To Agnes,

my sister, my confidant, my friend,
for all the wonderful years we shared...
in our times of joy, and of sorrow...
but most of all,
for all the memories you gave me.

You are in my prayers--*Always...*

Introduction...

I have reached my eighty-third year due only to a very benevolent God who has gifted me with good health, a sound mind, and the riches of a memory filled with seventy-nine years of wonderful experiences. The following are my recollections (verified by my editors) of an age and an era, and the realities of what life was like... how we lived, worked, sacrificed--and survived.

For my sister, Agnes, and me, life was what it was--two surviving children out of four born to our parents who provided for us as best they could during the Depression years and those that followed.

Our lives were humble and unadorned; proper and dignified. It was how the majority of us lived during the 1920s and '30s and through World War II when the norms of life and living changed.

I have always loved history. My years as an antique dealer and licensed appraiser afforded me an awareness of events as reflected in old newspapers and magazines, and in photographs and letters by those who lived in earlier years, as well as those in which Agnes and I lived. I also took note of those who directly or indirectly impacted so many souls throughout the last century.

I mention popular songs throughout the years because music was the one form of entertainment that has always been the thread binding my memories. The music of my youth represented the *essence of emotion* which has left an enduring sense of reflection.

This, then, is my *fidelity* to the times in which my sister and I lived; to those hard, but simpler years, when children respected parents as authority figures... when husbands and wives were faithful *until death do us part...* when money was scarce but a dollar was worth a whole hundred pennies, and when morality was the norm instead of the exception.

Agnes has passed on and I am left with my memories of how our lives began; how we grew into womanhood, fell in love, were blessed with children of our own, and how we were part of the end of an era that is no more and may never come again...

Part One

The 1920s

During the decade of the Twenties, statistics painted a picture of the United States with a population of over one-hundred-million people, an unemployment rate of 5%, and an average family income of about $1,200 a year.

While "the rich got richer, and the poor got poorer," by the end of the decade, very few people were *Putting on the Ritz.* One popular song of the time was, "*Yes, We Have No Bananas Today.*" Unfortunately, there were a great many things--in addition to bananas--the People didn't have on a great many days.

Construction began on the Empire State Building in New York City, but the skyscraper would not be completed until 1931, when I was nine and Agnes was seven.

The Era in which Agnes and I were born has been called *The Lost Generation* and *The Roaring 20s Generation* for those who came of age following World War I, as our parents had. It was a time that always intrigued me.

Historians have written how many from that generation were disillusioned and cynical, even contemptuous of the moral and proper way their parents' generation lived. At my age now, I have come to realize that each generation produces its own "renegades" who spend their lives asking: *Why Was I Born... Why Am I Living*, as one of the songs from the 1920s questioned.

The Lost Generation produced a wide dichotomy of personalities; from George Patton, Alfred Hitchcock, and Al Jolson; to Dwight D. Eisenhower, Adlai Stevenson, and Humphrey Bogart, among others.

Relying on scattered memories and my own years of research, I recall that the decade was a time that demeaned women with slang terms such as: "dame" or "broad" or, worse still, "charity girl," for sexually promiscuous women. It was the "flapper" era when women were in a state of transition, as motion pictures and magazines presented them with pastel painted faces, wearing boyish hairstyles and short tight skirts over gaunt figures.

Many other women of those years, including our Mother, wore ankle-length dresses with high necklines, but without distinguishing waistlines. While make-up products made their debut in the marketplace, our Mother never wore any. Her peaches-and-cream complexion and soft blue eyes, the color of a robin's egg, would have appeared terribly artificial.

Our Mother came of age in that *Lost Generation* and was not only strict, but an incredibly moral woman. With hindsight, those years had to have impacted her in far more serious ways than we realized.

At nineteen, Margaret Mary Tiernan stepped aboard the Cunard's *Oceanic* in Liverpool, England, took her place in steerage, and prayed that the good Lord would grant all souls on board an uneventful trip across the Atlantic to America.

The internal strife from decades of warring Catholic and Protestant factions had driven thousands of Ireland's young to seek religious freedom and new lives in America. They were but one nationality of the millions from across Europe, Russia, and Asia who left family and home for the country of unprecedented liberty and opportunity.

It was Columbus Day, October 12, 1904, after the incessant heat below deck, tainted food, and seasickness, that our Mother and eight other young Irish colleens were greeted by two nuns of the Dominican Order, their sponsoring authority for entry into the United States. Procedures required that immigrants be detained at Ellis Island for medical examinations and orientations. Following a short detention period, the young girls were sent to Dayton, Ohio where they were trained in spiritual or caregiving professions. Many became teachers for parochial schools; nurses for hospitals; or caregivers for children in orphanages or the sick and elderly in homes.

She accepted God's will and took a position as a nurse's assistant in a hospital, then became a caregiver to children in an orphanage.

Fourteen years of medical education and training placed our Mother among the ranks of those desperately needed following the end of World War I. She left Dayton, returned to New York and took up residency with an order of nursing nuns in Putnam County, New York, to care for the sick, maimed, and dying who came home from the War.

When immigrants arrived at Ellis Island, there was no mistaking the fact that they came to America because they wanted to *be* Americans. Today, immigrants are neither detained nor examined for communicable diseases. After living in our Country and benefiting from our form of government, a vast majority remain resistant to learning our language and our customs. *We* are expected, cajoled, intimidated, insulted, and forced to nullify *our* customs, holidays, and practices by the "politically correct" crowd, government officials, and the courts. What will our Country become? Will future generations even recognize it as the America we have known?

Our father, Walter James Griffin, was the only son of a German-Irish mother (a nurse) and Scottish father (medical student), both of whom worked at Bellevue Hospital in Manhattan. Dad's father died when he was two years old, in 1892, from a case of pneumonia. His grandfather wasted no time traveling to New York to demand that his grandson be turned over to him to raise. Dad's mother refused.

Six years later, grandfather Griffin returned to New York City insisting that our Dad leave his mother and return with him to Halifax, Nova Scotia. In addition to the original promise of a one-hundred dollar inheritance, he offered the best schooling available, and training to become a mariner. Dad refused!

He told us about his grandfather, Captain James Griffin, an insufferably stern and domineering Master Mariner, who left his home in Kirkholm, Scotland for a life at sea when only a thirteen-year-old boy. As Dad said, "Grandfather lived a very colorful life, indeed."

The Captain sailed schooners for Salter & Twining from the Port of Halifax during the mid-1800s. His ship carried supplies from England to all the ports on the Eastern seaboard, continued on to the Caribbean Islands where he took on hemp, sugar cane, and such, then sailed back up the coast unloading supplies at all of the same ports.

During the Civil War, Halifax became known as the "City of Treason," primarily because of their Southern sympathies and the amount of trading done with the South. When the Civil War broke out, it was inevitable that Captain Griffin would become one of those infamous blockade runners, sailing under cover of night, risking the lives of his crew, to bring embargoed supplies into the South.

The Captain had also mastered some of the first steam ships for the Cunard Line (which originated in Halifax), before his death in 1901. I remember the many times Agnes had said how she wished we could have known the Captain. I know she inherited some of his wanderlust.

Our Dad attended St. Colomba's Grammar School in Manhattan where he was an altar boy and member of the boys choir, both of which he had been enormously proud. Unfortunately, a bout with Scarlet Fever resulted in a punctured eardrum which interrupted his choir participation. He graduated from the prestigious Catholic Christian Brothers High School, also in Manhattan. When World War I broke out, he attempted to enlist but none of the branches of service would take him due to his hearing problem.

Of all the jobs Dad could have had, he chose to be a stage hand with the Ziegfeld Follies in New York City. I remember the countless stories he told of his days backstage watching Eddie Cantor, W.C. Fields, and Ziegfeld's leading ladies, Fannie Brice, Billie Burke, and Marilynn Miller.

He loved the opulence of the New Amsterdam Theater where Florenz Ziegfeld produced his Follies from 1913 through the Twenties. We found copies of the Programs he had kept from the Theater; their covers boldly lettered on a field of deep forest green in ornate Art Nouveau designs. Agnes and I wondered how grand it must have been to have dressed up and been a part of the theater life.

Dad loved photography so it was no surprise that he had been intrigued with the early film makers. For a short time, he worked for Fox, which had studios in Ft. Lee, across the Hudson River in New Jersey. Had fate dealt Dad another hand, he might have stayed with Fox and moved to Hollywood. Instead, he met Margaret Mary Tiernan and fell in love. They married in January 1921 in St. Columba's Roman Catholic Church in Lower Manhattan, where Dad had been an altar boy.

The year before they married gave way to the enactment of the Volstead Act under the Eighteenth Amendment that banned the sale of alcohol. I mention this in light of the "excuses" our parents told us the government and others had used to justify the prohibition of liquor.

Some had said that the flood of Irish, Italian, German, and Jewish immigrants presented a threat to the socio-economic balance within the U.S., *because their traditions had embraced alcohol*. Our Mother said that she was particularly enraged by the prejudicial thinking which served only to stereotype those immigrants as drinkers who, allegedly, could not be trusted and who would probably bring crime and violence to others in the country.

There were also those who had fantasized that the Volstead Act was needed to *improve the economy* and the *quality of life* by *reducing crime and poverty*. (Today, however, we're faced not only with illegal immigrants, but with *terrorists* posing as--and using--immigrants to enter our Country. Yet, our borders remain open and unprotected and we haven't seen one piece of legislation to stop the flood of illegal immigrants--have we?)

Prohibition "improved the economy and the quality of life" all right--*for gangsters* and *their crooked political allies.* It also significantly *increased* crime from coast to coast and border to border because Prohibition created an unprecedented underground economy. Bootleggers serviced thousands of speakeasies--siphoning millions of dollars from the Nation's economy. The Volstead Act had created a tax-free, multi-million dollar industry for Al Capone, Dutch Schultz, the *Mob* around the country, along with their political allies, which most people never learned about until years later.

The *decade of plenty,* indeed, had been filled with *plenty* of gangsters and crooked politicians who couldn't (or wouldn't) control the tidal wave of murder and mayhem.

After all the years I have lived, I've come to the conclusion that our "elected representatives" pass *laws* (wearing blinders and earplugs), often worsening the problems their laws were "alleged" to fix.

Before the 1930s, the government stayed out of the People's business and lives. There were very few government programs that provided financial assistance--or welfare--especially for the immigrants of the Twenties. There were, however, churches, the Salvation Army, the Insane Asylum, and orphanages--all of which carried the burden of providing for those who had neither home nor money to survive. The People were in constant fear with the ever-present thought: "*I don't want to wind up in the Poor House!*"

I arrived on October 4, 1922, when Jazz also threatened to bring down American society, and The Ku Klux Klan--long dormant following the Civil War's Reconstruction period-- reemerged to control Catholics, Jews, Blacks, and drunkards who beat their wives and children.

Susie was Eddie Cantor's hit song that year, while Al Jolson gave the Country *Toot Toot Tootsie, Goo'Bye,* and Babe Ruth was America's sports darling as the highest paid baseball player in the game.

Magazines and newspapers conditioned the masses with enticing and colorful full-page advertisements that had everyone wishing and wanting to own everything that was offered. Door-to-door salesmen canvassed neighborhoods hawking their newly developed products to the People who believed their own financial worth could only get better. The People spent freely and enjoyed the new and revolutionary products that promised an easier lifestyle.

Radio inundated the masses with repetitious sales campaigns for soaps, hair products, and the like. As one advertisement put it, if you didn't gargle with *Listerine* before every social occasion, you'd never get any invitations and wind up friendless!

I remember one magazine advertisement depicting a girl standing on the dance floor in her glamorous evening dress, beside her date under a moonlit sky--it was when *you absolutely better have used Mum* (deodorant), so that your date wouldn't elevate his nose in the air, excuse himself, and leave you on the dance floor alone(!)

Americans were tempted with a *new* kind of freedom guaranteed to give them endless mobility with a *new automobile*. A new Ford was only two-hundred-ninety dollars; gasoline was only ten cents a gallon, pumped by a smiling, uniformed station attendant who washed your windshield and checked the car's water and oil levels. There was only one grade of gasoline back then--and it came from *America's* oil fields.

Dance marathons became the rage and, of course, everyone was in awe of Harry Houdini, the man who mesmerized the masses with his death-defying escape antics.

Life was good and getting better following "*The War to end all Wars*," as World War I had been called. Even though Communism had been considered a growing threat, nothing could stop *The Lost Generation* who were beginning to live the good life--Prohibition, or no Prohibition.

My sister, Agnes, was born in Manhattan on January 2, 1924. It was a year for the South with songs like: *Alabamy Bound, Call of the South,* and *Arkansas Blues*, though I personally don't remember them. George and Ira Gershwin gave the Country *Fascinating Rhythm, The Man I Love,* and *Oh, Lady Be Good.*

It was the year Vladimir Lenin, head of the fledgling Union of Soviet Socialist Republics, died. Leon Trotsky and Josef Stalin, two diametrically opposed Communists, were left to rule the Soviet Union.

America still had not become a *Dry Nation,* as the People were led to believe. They saw increasing numbers of gangsters and gangland killings. What they didn't see were the numbers of corrupt politicians and police who were unable to deny themselves a share of the millions being made from the failed law and *The Prisoner's Song* seemed all too appropriate as 1924 came to an end.

Three of our Mother's brothers were some of New York City's *finest* policemen and two were firemen who, along with fellow officers, bemoaned the corruption but were helpless to do anything to stop it.

Our baby brother, Robert Emmett, was also born in Manhattan on April 12, 1925 but tragically died three months later in July. That was the year of the *Summer Complaint*, the name for the illness that killed untold numbers of children as a result of contaminated milk while the politicians' attentions were fixed on the flow of illegal liquor.

The Scopes Monkey Trial in Dayton, Tennessee was a major event in 1926, as our Dad told us much later. He said the trial had taken center stage with the first ever nationally broadcast radio coverage of the controversial trial. Our staunch Irish Catholic mother, as well as most Bible-believing people, viewed the trial very seriously.

Our Dad said he had been particularly concerned when he learned that the American Civil Liberties Union had appointed attorney Clarence Darrow--known to have been a socialist who had defended labor, the oppressed, *and* big business--to represent John Thomas

Scopes, the teacher who defied the law to teach Darwin's theory that man evolved from the monkey.

William Jennings Bryan--the devout Bible-quoting Christian who was against all that was contrary to the Bible--represented the State of Tennessee. The evidence was clear: Scopes had blatantly violated the law under the Butler Act that upheld the Bible's teaching of creation. Scopes was found guilty and received a one-hundred-dollar fine. It was a clear message to anyone who wanted to further the theory of evolution--the *law* meant nothing, and the "punishment" confirmed it.

While countless magazine articles, television productions, and a Hollywood movie have fashioned their perspectives of the Monkey Trial, I can only convey our parents' views: Mom saw an anti-God, anti-Bible agenda, while Dad saw a movement hellbent on creating a society without any absolute beliefs. (I am reminded of George Santayana's view that: "Those who ignore history are doomed to repeat it." I also happen to agree with his notion that history is a "pack of lies" told by "people who weren't there.")

The freewheeling attitudes and tumultuous events of those times gave our Mother pause that her daughters would need strict supervision, along with an unalterable set of values and unyielding moral character. I recall her telling me (on more than one occasion) how very precocious I was as a child, though I had been mindful and very obedient. She decided that we should move out of Manhattan. Perhaps her real purpose was to escape the sadness that surrounded her in our apartment where little Robert Emmett had died.

As it turned out, it had been a pragmatic move because our Dad was employed by the Public Service Power & Light Company of New Jersey at their branch office in Englewood. It was also practical because our parents owned the piece of property that Dad's mother had purchased in 1900 (with his one-hundred dollar inheritance from the Captain). Grandma Griffin had given the property to our parents as a wedding gift.

The property was located about a mile outside of the Englewood city limits in West Englewood, on a street called Manhattan Avenue.

It seemed like a picture postcard; a wooded wonderland with overhanging branches of maple and chestnut trees, weeping willows, peach, quince, and apple trees spotting the landscape. It cradled us in a fragrant and peaceful solace that set our lives on a course which, as I now reflect, was part of destiny.

Englewood was re-developing a small neighborhood that had a tract of houses which were being sold below market value with the proviso that the new owners had to relocate the houses to their own property. Our parents purchased one of those houses, and our Mother set out early one morning to conclude the arrangements for its move.

She took a taxi to the Hudson Ferry Line for the short river crossing to the New Jersey side where she boarded the trolley in Leonia that brought her to the Dean Street and Palisade Avenue in Englewood. She walked to Armory Street expecting to see the house, but found only strapped bundles of lumber and stacks of windows and doors piled on the empty lot where the little house had stood only days before.

She frantically raced to City Hall and was told that first, permits had to be obtained, a foundation on her Manhattan Avenue property had to be dug, a truck would be required to transport the disassembled house and, of course, the utilities would have to be connected. Mom broke down in tears as she stood on the steps of City Hall overwhelmed by the daunting task and how it would ever be accomplished.

Sitting on those steps was an older gentleman, Mr. Louis Wurm who, upon seeing our Mother crying, said. "Ma'am, is there something wrong? Is there some help you need?" She explained the situation and, to her surprise, the gentleman said, "Ma'am, have your husband here tomorrow morning and I'll see what I can do to help."

The next morning, our parents drove to Englewood. Louie Wurm and three other men were waiting on the steps of City Hall. It took several trips for them to load and unload the bundles of wood, windows and doors. Over the course of several weeks, they dug out a foundation, connected the water and sewer lines, and reconstructed the old house. There were no building plans so, in all probability, the old house may not have been rebuilt as originally constructed.

I turned four in the autumn of 1926; Agnes was two, and we were living in West Englewood, New Jersey. In my mind's eye, I see a beautifully bright and tranquil day and my Mother kneeling down to me holding a half of a bologna sandwich that she breaks in half again and hands to me. I can see the clover in the green patch beside me, as I think back to my first memory of our "new" home which wasn't new at all, but which had been built sometime in the late 1870's.

Back then, our little house was called a "cottage" which, years later, became known as a "bungalow." It had four rooms and, as we were told, sat in a little neighborhood of similar homes for people who had worked for one of the larger companies in Englewood.

Our parents continually upgraded the house, including a new kitchen and a laundry room that ran the full width of the back of the house, as well as a front sun room with four twelve-light windows that welcomed Spring's scented breezes, and allowed us to eavesdrop on Autumn's play with the falling leaves.

Despite our father's position with the power company, he could not get them to set the power poles and run the electrical line to the house so, during the winter months, coal stoves in the kitchen and living room provided heat, and decorative kerosene lamps illuminated the rooms with a soft radiance that made everything seem cozy and perfect. Cooking was done on the coal stove in the kitchen.

The reality, which never occurred to me as a little girl, was that our parents had taken a small, unadorned cottage that had been built in the late eighteen-hundreds and, with much love and care, had "modernized" it with Twentieth Century upgrades.

Occasionally, young people have asked me: *How did you ever manage?*

Our way of life seems incomprehensible to today's generations who have been inundated with so many technologically-advanced conveniences, but the simple truth is that we couldn't have missed what we never had, anymore than we could have realized how different life could be with the conveniences of a later time.

Those early years were filled with innovative products and conveniences... Businessmen and vacationers saw hotel advertisements for "Your home away from home with a *radio in every room,*" along with ads that read: "Running Water! A necessity! with the Hoosier pressurized water pump and tank. And, *"You can enjoy city plumbing out beyond the sewer line,"* with the new San-Equip septic tanks.

Our parents bought a Nesco Oil Cook Stove they saw advertised in a magazine: *"It fries, bakes, broils, boils, toasts clean, and can simmer. One burner burns 25 hours on a gallon of kerosene,"* as the ad boasted. The stove was made of white porcelain with a pea green trim. Our Mother, subsequently, painted the kitchen walls in green to match the trim, accentuating the white woodwork and cabinets.

Shortly afterward, a hot-air furnace was purchased and placed in the basement. I remember Agnes and I played near the metal grate in the center of the living room floor, enjoying the way the warm air blew up into our faces.

In early Spring of 1927, a few months after we had moved into the house, the Power & Light Company finally heeded Dad's requests and erected tall poles topped off with huge cross arms and insulators from which electrical wires connected to our house on Manhattan Avenue. I remember so many afternoon walks in the snow with my baby sister, Agnes, and our parents and seeing our cottage at the end of the block, that seemed a glowing beacon in the woodland haunt.

As we all settled into our new home, Dad began to learn about the early beginnings of Englewood and of its significance in history which, of course, he loved. As I share with you our continuing connection with Manhattan, I want to say that Englewood is only three miles west of the George Washington Bridge, and only ten miles from Times Square. Even though these short distances seem inconsequential now because of people's mobility and the super highways, it wasn't always easy for us to get into the City. Few buses ran from Englewood into Manhattan, and ferries were the primary means of transportation across the Hudson River.

The little town of Englewood sits in a valley at the foot of the western slope of the Palisades, a rocky cliff line that borders the western shore of the Hudson River, named for Henry Hudson who sailed up the waterway in 1607.

Unfortunately, the Hackensack tribe of the Lenape Indians, were driven from the land by the early Dutch immigrants who Hudson allowed to settle on his land claim. The Dutch were joined by French Huguenots and English émigrés. And, of all Englewood's rich history, there is no greater prominence than having been the town to which General George Washington escaped when the British troops tried to entrap him at Ft. Lee, New Jersey. Had Washington not been able to escape the British forces, the Revolutionary War could easily have ended in Englewood with Washington's surrender at the corner of Palisade Avenue and Tenafly Road where his headquarters stood in 1780.

Englewood's history documents Washington's departure from the little town as he led his troops up *Liberty Road*, escaping the British troops.

There was a little room under the peak of the roof in the attic where Agnes and I could be found playing and investigating the things that remained packed after our move from Manhattan. As the years passed, Agnes and I grew even more intrigued with the *treasures* hidden away in crates. We spent hours reading the stories in Dad's *Liberty Boy* magazines about the Revolutionary War, staring at the covers that were full lithograph drawings of young boys wearing the garb of 1776 patriots. How their images piqued our imaginations, which our Dad enhanced with his own stories about our country's early history and the town in which we lived. He stirred our thoughts with his wonderful stories about history and his tales of little Englewood, the Lenape Indians, and the sailing ships that had crossed the Atlantic.

He and his Kodak camera--the kind with the glass plates that became the negatives--were inseparable. He used the little place in the attic as his dark room where Agnes and I patiently waited in the glow of a red bulb, watching as he carefully placed those glass panes into a pan of water then, holding the glass frames up to the light, how they *magically* produced the reverse images of what became our childhood photographs.

Our primary sources for news and entertainment during the late Twenties were newspapers and a battery-operated radio our parents had purchased. It was cheaper than the electric models and held us spellbound as curious voices and music came through the square black box with wires that had to be grounded to a metal object.

Agnes was three, I was four, as 1927 got underway. I remember that there were very few radio stations and an awful lot of static that made what was being said difficult to hear. Those early years held no where near the variety of entertainment that exists today; yet, we were happy with the few but good things that came our way.

At the end of our Dad's long work day, he would bring each of us a little bag of peanuts and nonpareil candies, the chocolate disks with tiny white candy dots on top; or *MaryJanes* from Woolworth's in downtown Englewood. Occasionally, his pole inspector friend, John Rhome or, "Rommy" as Dad nicknamed him, would stop by to discuss the politics of the day.

How clearly I remember Rommy--a restless sort who preferred to stand rather than sit, and who always chewed on his pipe while Mom perked a pot of coffee in her white porcelain coffee maker. Sometimes he leaned against the icebox that held the twenty-five-cent block of ice that had to be replaced three times a week to keep food from spoiling.

Charles Lindbergh, or *Lucky Lindy* as he was affectionately named, had flown his specially-designed plane, the *Spirit of St. Louis,* 3,610 miles from St. Louis across the Atlantic to Paris in thirty-three-and-a-half hours on May 21, 1927. It had been the first ever crossing of its kind and resulted in a ticker-tape parade in New York City, the likes of which any politician would forever envy. He was our national hero, the most popular man in America and the crowning glory of all that America represented. I remember the grown-ups talking about him, and the pride they held for America's daring aviator.

That was before the Good Lord blessed our parents with Alexander Louis, who was born at home on June 29, 1927. A French lady assisted Doctor Irwin, the attending physician. As I think back to that day, I have the brief sense and feeling that Dad kept Agnes and me preoccupied and sheltered from the birthing event.

Though only three-years-old, Agnes thought of our new baby brother as her living *doll*. Almost five years of age and the oldest sibling, I seemed to know that I had a new responsibility, in addition to watching over and playing with Agnes which, on occasion, I thought was a nuisance. I loved to sit in the chair rocking and listening to the music on the radio. Of course, being the *first* child, I suppose I had the feeling that I was going to take another back seat to yet another new arrival. For the eldest child, there is no disputing the suggestion of sibling rivalry in all of its unexpected ramifications.

Mom would always say, "Go play with yer sister..." Agnes was just a three-year old toddler and every bit as insistent as our Mother, saying, "Let's dress them up and have our tea..." She talked to the wide-eyed composition headed dolls as little girls do, and dressed them in their tiny clothes herself. Although only fifteen months separated us and because Mom tasked me with the responsibility of looking after my little sister, I considered myself much bigger than Agnes.

Our Dad put in long, hard hours while Mom's almost endless days were filled with tending to the shopping, maintaining our home, planting vegetables in our garden, and caring for three children. There was nothing exceptional about our lives, we lived as other families had and yet, I remember those less fortunate people who had fallen under harder times, and how they could always count on Mom for some hot food, and a good dose of religion.

Though I had just turned seven years old that October of the Wall Street *Crash* in 1929, I remember the long discussions during which our parents talked about what might happen to us. Yet, through all their fears and trepidation, they remained hopeful--and prayed.

Much has been written about the personal disasters of that October day and the desperate months that followed. It seemed that there was nothing anyone could do to stop the country's spiral into the *Great* Depression. The Country was imploding--No, it was disintegrating--as if some inexplicable, catastrophic disease had seized our country. We had experienced nearly a decade of prosperity, despite the folly of Prohibition and gangland wars. Through it all, newspapers and radio commentators continued to report that "it" would pass and "everything would be fine."

Those early impressions had been nothing more than, as Dad described them, empty words of spoon-fed propaganda. He had a remarkable political acumen, always sharing his perspectives on the Depression and his sense that it had a "purpose" -- one the country didn't suspect until much later.

He felt fairly secure in his position as a Public Service inspector yet, while nobody could feel totally confident that their jobs would last due to mounting layoffs which led to record-breaking unemployment, Dad continued to provide.

John B. Gambling of WOR Radio opened his morning *Rambling with Gambling* show with: *Look for the Silver Lining...For somewhere the sun is shining,* as everybody scurried and hurried to have a bit of breakfast; scrambled eggs and buttered toast for Agnes and me before we left for school; a fried egg sandwich for Dad. I knew the *sun was shining* and everyone else knew the *sun was shining*, I just wondered *how* a "silver lining" could possibly make anything better.

I have so many fond memories of John B. Gambling and of his daily commitment to inspire the thousands of us who were a little less depressed as we set out for yet another day into the unknown.

Christmas 1929 brought a big shiny red and green metal truck for Alexander and two great big dolls--one for Agnes and one for me. They were sitting on doll chairs at a little table with a tea service for four. They were identical, except one doll was dressed in blue and one in pink. I got the one dressed in blue, and the feeling lingers that I might have been a little disappointed-- although I can't say for sure--to tell the truth, I really didn't like dolls as a little girl.

PART TWO

The 1930s

The decade of the Thirties ushered in the *Great* Depression to a U.S. population of over 123,000,000 people whose annual family income averaged $1,300. Today, that would unquestionably qualify a person for *the poor house,* or an extended stay in an institution.

The unemployment rate was reported at 25% and *Singin' In The Rain* and *Sunny Side Up* failed to inspire. Imagine 31,750,000 people without any viable source of income which resulted in homelessness. Milk was fourteen cents a quart; bread was nine cents a loaf, and round steak was forty-two cents a pound for those who could afford it and, those who could afford it were usually at the top of the economic ladder humming *You Were Meant For Me.*

Over the years, as I came across the word "*Great*" attached to the Depression, I paused and asked why the word *Great* was used, instead of *colossal* or *monstrous.* (It did impact the world.) To have used the word "Great" conjures suspicion that the Depression may have been *celebrated* for having achieved some incredible *fete accompli* -- as the *Great* Locomotive Chase, or the *Great* Santini; you get the general idea.

The Star Spangled Banner was officially designated as our national anthem in 1931. In hindsight, *Brother, Can You Spare a Dime?* would have been more appropriate...

"They used to tell me I was building a dream
And so I followed the mob
When there was earth to plow or guns to bear
I was always there right on the job
They used to tell me I was building a dream
With peace and glory ahead
Why should I be standing in line
Just waiting for bread?"
(lyrics by Yip Harburg, music by Gorney Harburg)

By the end of the decade, Kate Smith introduced Irving Berlin's *God Bless America* which everyone in the country had already been asking God to do because Wall Street and Washington had pretty much fouled up enough to last decades.

I am not an economist and don't profess to be one. I just know from experience that those who can't play the big boys' game should stay out of it. In fact, I seem to recall Dad telling me that John D. Rockefeller had the same view.

I believed then, as I continue to believe today, that the people had been swept up in the prosperity of the Twenties and lulled into the euphoria of a never-ending supply of everything--until *everything* began to evaporate. Public schools closed because the people had lost their jobs and couldn't pay their taxes, they couldn't buy food and clothing, or pay their mortgage installments.

Of course, there was Hollywood.

Moviemakers had done their damnedest to defy traditional values, the accepted norms of morality, and showed little respect for the law. Hollywood's version of morals, and its contempt for religion and the law, triggered a public outcry until Will H. Hays, (former chairman of the Republican National Committee, former Postmaster General, and president of the Motion Picture Producers and Distributors of America) stepped in with what was called the *Hays Office* and his "Code."

The *Hays' Code* had set standards and guidelines regarding Hollywood's treatment of sex, violence and crime, as well as their inappropriate views toward religion. While Hollywood's filmmakers agreed to accept the Hays Code in 1930, they didn't implement it until 1934. They agreed *not* to exploit sex and violence, and would refrain from their anti-religious bent under a *forty year moratorium* which would have ended in 1970. (As we've seen since the 1960s, sex and violence are sellable commodities, while God is not. The *free love* and marijuana-laced mentality of the Sixties closed the door on morality as we knew it. If the People wake up, I believe the pendulum can be made to swing back, returning us to morality and decency again.)

By the end of the Thirties, Hollywood had given the world the exceptionally talented Shirley Temple; the South's version of the "War Between the States" from Margaret Mitchell's *Gone With The Wind;* the escapism and magic of *The Wizard of Oz,* and the forever grace, dignity, and charm of Ginger Rogers and Fred Astaire--all phenomenal moneymakers. One Hollywood producer gave the people John Steinbeck's view of the *Great* Depression with *The Grapes of Wrath.*

Glenn Miller, Tommy and Jimmy Dorsey, and Benny Goodman, to name a few band leaders, gave Agnes and me and thousands of teenagers like us, the *Big Bands*, which made our hearts light, in spite of the *Great* Depression.

Radio news commentators of our day were nothing like the *talk radio* hosts of today--with one exception: Charles E. Coughlin (like Rush Limbaugh) amassed a national audience that faithfully tuned-in for his weekly broadcast throughout the 1930s. The Catholic priest from Chicago sermonized and provided political commentary on the times, exercising his freedom of speech, which FDR enjoyed during his early years in office, but which became an *aggravation* by the end of the decade.

Edward R. Murrow, H.V. Kaltenborn and Gabriel Heater were also commentators of the time, each with his own "spin" and style of reporting. Jimmy Fiddler and Walter Winchell disclosed the titillating news of the *kings and queens* of Hollywood and Broadway.

Happy Days Are Here Again, a popular song from the 1930s, was lively and uplifting, and momentarily seized the senses. For me, reality soon overrode the song's mind-altering euphoria--there were no *happy days* in the Thirties. The Democrats appropriated the tune which I considered an affront to the vast majority of the "working class" who could only hope and pray that FDR's *fireside chats* were more than "feel-good" bibble-babble.

Through all of the hardships of the Thirties, it must be said that there was some Federal assistance managed by the states and which filtered down to the county and city levels. However, as I grew older, I thought the "uppity governing elite" saw the need to fill their plates a little more than the rest of the People. It made me wonder exactly whose plate got filled *first.*

There were virtually no significant cases of rapes, robberies or murders (except those within the gangsters' world). Abortion was a *crime* and no doctor (with ethics and a valid license) would be a party to destroying unborn life as their Hippocratic Oath forbid. Regardless of what some "back-alley" payoff might have been--IF the people had the money to pay for one--there was a prison term awaiting the "butcher" who performed an abortion.

I don't remember any girls throughout our school years who behaved improperly. However, if a girl was promiscuous and became pregnant, she was immediately taken out of school and sent to live with a relative in another city or state and the baby was either given up for adoption or kept by a relative to raise. In spite of the hardships of the times and all of the babies who had died of natural causes or tainted milk, life was sacred and the majority of people moral.

1930

The year following the *Stock Market Crash*, unemployment inched up to 8.9% causing President Herbert Hoover to appoint an Unemployment Relief Commission. Undoubtedly, there were some who preferred he sang a different *Three Little Words* while Hoover probably wanted to name names as *Sing, You Sinners* played on the radio.

One wintery evening in 1930, I remember my lackluster attempt at washing the supper dishes as the radio announcer introduced Guy Lombardo and His Royal Canadians who began playing. *I'm Confessin' That I Love You.* I was standing at the kitchen sink, running my fingers under the hot water, dabbling, and daydreaming about the song. I felt a tug on my dress as six-year-old Agnes stood beside me and asked, "Margaret, why would anyone have to confess that they love someone?"

As young as she was, Agnes always seemed to ask the most thought-provoking questions, many of which I couldn't answer to her satisfaction. I came to realize that while she seemed not to be paying attention, she never missed much.

Radio programming became more diverse with shows like the half-hour mystery, *The Shadow*, portrayed by Alonzo Dean Cole who also acted out *The Witch's Tale,* and both of which I loved. They were scary, but I liked the eerie sounds and couldn't wait for each Monday night's episode of *The Witch's Tale*. Light bulbs weren't nearly as bright as they have been for the last half century and so, our dimly-lit living room seemed to incubate the perfect mood for *The Witch's Tale* and *The Shadow.*

Agnes wasn't fond of either show and her weekly request: "I don't like that scary thing, Mama," fell on deaf ears as we all sat around for the next installments.

I know that all summer long I had dreaded the start of school. Our parents had insisted that I wait to start school when Agnes did. I was about to turn eight, nearly two years advanced of all the other first graders and wondered: *Would the other children know that I was a year-and-a-half older than they?* While I don't remember our very first day at St. Cecelia's Catholic School in Englewood, I do know that it had been the last day in September. Parochial schools, as private schools, usually set their own rules and regulations, as St. Cecelia's had been doing since 1872.

After my first week, I realized that I truly did love school. I was intrigued with just about everything that was taught, except for the *Dick and Jane* books which introduced a new word on each page. Our Dad had been teaching us how to read for some time so, I felt I needed something more challenging than *Dick and Jane*. I was a good student, as was Agnes, and in a few short months, the principal advanced me to second grade. Six-year old Agnes remained in first grade, delighted to be rid of me, knowing that I couldn't tattletale on her if she misbehaved.

Autumn, especially October, has always been my favorite time of the year thus, it seems appropriate that I should recall our first Halloween party. It was a fun day. The Sisters had filled a metal tub with water--so the children could *bob for apples* by challenging the children to seize an apple in their teeth. Their smiling wet faces dripped little puddles of water all over the wide-planked wood floors. I thought it messy and inappropriate. I was the prissy type. I didn't *bob*, I watched.

Then Agnes' teacher, Sister Catherine Pierre, tied a string to the stem of an apple and gently swung it back and forth as she instructed four or five little people to gather around and try to sink their teeth into it. The victorious one would win a prize. Agnes had the most fun trying to catch that swinging apple. This, too, was more fun to watch than to attempt. I was an observer, not a participant, prize or no prize.

The next day was the first of November, the Feast of All Saints Day, a holy day of obligation, requiring all Roman Catholic adults and children to attend Mass.

Sister Catherine Pierre was a great role model for Agnes and me. Her influence resulted in our play acting that we were teachers, just like our Nuns. I would hold a stick, pointing to an imaginary blackboard as my teacher, Sister Margaret Lawrence, had done while calling out to the *naughty* children in the classroom. Sometimes, we pretended we were standing in a hall and Agnes would point into the imaginary classroom, imitating her teacher and saying, "Behave yourselves, children. We know who's making the disturbance." Little Alexander loved the funny faces and stern way Agnes spoke to our make-believe children.

I remember that one of our neighbors wasn't especially happy to see us running around as "nuns" with black crepe veils on our heads. It was no secret to anyone that he didn't like children and, it wasn't long before we found out that he wasn't particularly fond of Catholics either.

Breakfast was an important meal never to be missed; supper, on the other hand, had particular significance. It was our time for sharing what we learned in school. Dad always found a way to advance our learning with stories that made what we were taught even more exciting. Alexander giggled hysterically as he watched Agnes' silly faces, knowing enough to laugh each time Agnes laughed at one of our Dad's stories.

I recall so many evenings sitting at the kitchen table, our Mother feeding Alexander the baby food she had prepared for him, and we eating our portions of the Icy Point Salmon she had divided into four parts, along with string beans, potatoes, and a slice of whole wheat bread.

She was a devoted listener of *McCann's Pure Food Hour*, hosted by Alfred McCann, the nutritionist who broadcast over WOR Radio during the Twenties. His broadcasts were "revolutionary" in the way he talked about the need to eat natural foods, which were so much more nutritious, although our Mother had learned a great deal about natural remedies and herbs while training with the nuns.

"Natural" foods weren't the commercialized (or "suspect") products they've become over the last few decades and pharmaceutical houses were not intimidated by those promoting natural products.

With the high cost of prescriptions, I can't understand why the pharmaceutical houses spend the millions of dollars they do advertising to the *public.* The public can't buy the drugs being advertised without doctors writing the prescriptions for them! Maybe, if they stopped spending those millions on advertising, they could make their drugs a whole lot cheaper for us.

Following Alfred McCann's death in 1931, son Alfred Jr., took over the show and continued educating the People about the need to eat natural foods rather than processed foods. A much larger selection of naturally-grown foods was available 75 years ago, very little of which was subjected to forced ripening or cold storage. We ate the fruits and vegetables of the season. We had cross-country shipping of produce, but produce from other states was always much higher priced and out of the reach of the average family, as it remains today.

Marge Griffin-Glausier

1931

Unemployment escalated to 16.3% and the song, *The Peanut Vendor*, gave rise to the possibility of a new profession for many of the growing unemployed.

Al Capone, Chicago's premier thug, was convicted and sentenced to eleven-years in prison for *tax evasion*, as if he had been the only one guilty of not paying taxes on his millions of illegally-earned dollars! Kate Smith, "The Songbird of the South", was introduced that year along with her theme song, *When The Moon Comes Over The Mountain*.

Church remained at the core of our family life, as it was for many in the community. There is no doubt in my mind that faith sustained the great majority of people during those years. The sex and violence Hollywood promulgated had not altered the vulnerability of society, despite the degree to which the public had been subjected to forces beyond their knowledge or control.

Three-and-a-half year-old Alexander, seven-year old Agnes, and I, at eight-and-a-half years, attended Sunday morning Mass with our parents. On Tuesday evenings we faithfully attended devotions to the Little Flower, the saint of modern times who had been canonized in 1927.

Twice a year, we attended a nine-day novena; one to the Blessed

Mother, and one to Saint Teresa. (A *"novena"* is the saying of prayers to a special saint to intercede to God on a penitent's behalf. Of course, we prayed to God, but having a little extra help couldn't hurt.)

On the last day of a novena, children who had not yet received their First Holy Communion wore garlands of dainty flowers and leaves on their heads. The elementary grade children would stand in a straight line and remain silent--as the Nuns had sternly instructed. Then we would march from the grammar school to the vestibule of the church where we again waited for the priest to lead off the procession, carrying the Blessed Sacrament. He slowly walked down one side of the aisle toward the altar, then up the other until he reached the massive oak doors at the rear of the church. He turned and proceeded down the wide center aisle to the altar where he began the opening prayers in Latin.

Each last evening of a novena would culminate with hymns of adoration and the priest's blessing. If God couldn't help us get through the hard times, then no one could, as Mom and Dad faithfully believed. I'm taking heart that Americans have been expressing their faith and have begun to counter those with no beliefs or values. The horrendous practice of situation ethics has been a cancer eating away at the very soul of our Nation. But then, evil will always rear its ugly head if we become complacent and stray, as Mom was always fond of saying.

Our Mother was the driving force which made our faith a natural part of who we were. We'd all walk to Englewood for the eight o'clock Mass, and afterward, we would walk back down James Street, passing all the beautiful Victorian homes that had been built prior to the turn-of-the-century, and then onto Palisade Avenue for our ritual stop at the bakery for a crumb cake or a tasty raisin danish ring with thick white icing.

We'd walk up West Palisade Avenue for home, stopping at Moe Liberman's, between James and West Streets, for the Sunday papers. Mr. Lieberman and his mother ran their confectionary store which offered a wide variety of candies, gum, magazines, and all of the New York newspapers. They also carried general sundry items which were displayed in slant-topped, glass display cases. We'd continue our walk home and Mom would prepare breakfast while Dad read us the *Katzenjammer Kids.*

In February, the newspapers reported that American inventor Thomas Edison had died. Dad, in his customary fashion, took the news and turned it into a learning lesson about all that Thomas Edison had invented and done for the people. Dad made certain to mention what he considered one of Edison's truly great inventions: *"the movie-making machine."*

May 1, 1931, was a *monumental* day. It marked the official opening of the tallest skyscraper in the country--The Empire State Building--all twelve-hundred-fifty feet. It had one-hundred-two floors, and a domed cap atop a two-hundred-fifty-foot tower that pierced the clouds above. It was a sight to behold among the other heretofore sky-high buildings of the time.

Two years later, the American people had the chance to see the skyscraper in the movie, *King Kong,* starring Fay Wray, Bruce Cabot, and Robert Armstrong. Hollywood had continued to cross the line with suggestive scenes and did cut those vulgar scenes out before releasing the movie. However, those scenes have since been added back into the original film, as if there was a need to have them in the movie in the first place.

One beautiful Sunday morning in May, Agnes and I received our First Holy Communion. It had been a very special day that began with a long procession of little girls dressed all in white, with veils perched on their heads. The little boys wore long white stockings under white knickers with white shirts, and jackets.

Our Mother baked a cake and Dad made the ice cream which, sadly, hadn't turned out exactly right because the homemade cranks and the freezer unit didn't work properly. If ice cream had been store bought, it would have to be eaten on the spot, right then and there, before it melted. Refrigeration was not as it is today.

Mom occasionally invited our school chums, Eleanor and Virginia, and their mother for lunch. I remember the four of us girls playing at the side of the house near the lilac bushes, picking flowers, giggling and acting silly as most young girls did.

We four had walked the mile to school in the mornings and, occasionally, Eleanor's mother would stop by to visit and enjoy Mom's famous biscuits or fruit cake, along with a pot of hot Salada or White Rose tea. During one of her visits, a disagreement erupted about some point of religion, as I recall. That was the end of our friendship with Eleanor and Virginia. Mom was stubbornly dogmatic and a more-than-willing spokesperson for the Roman Catholic faith--any place and every place--always.

On the last day of the school term in 1931, a considerable anxiousness and pride filled me as Agnes and I walked home to show our parents our report cards. It pleased them that Agnes had been promoted to second grade, and I to fourth grade. But then, they knew we would--or God Himself, would need to help us!

That summer also brought a severe outbreak of Polio, Infantile Paralysis as it was known then. The disease had me quite concerned; so concerned, in fact, that during the late afternoons in August and September, I would hurry down Palisade Avenue to Rusch's General Store for a copy of our local newspaper, *The Bergen Evening Record.* My fear compelled me to see what was being reported about the numbers of new cases of Infantile Paralysis and if it was spreading throughout Englewood and Teaneck. Thanks to God, the outbreak hadn't seized anyone we knew, though even one case would send panic up one's spine.

It wasn't uncommon for schools to remain closed until late in September when of the disease were reported.

One late summer day, when we were all playing in the yard, Mom found a hearty little maple tree in the woods next to our house. She dug up the tiny tree and Agnes and I helped her plant it next to the house. We sat on the narrow concrete walk while Dad made a tree swing that same afternoon. He bored two holes on each side of the wood plank that would be the seat, threaded a heavy rope through the holes and tied knots beneath the board. He then climbed up the towering chestnut tree, beyond where we had planted the tiny maple tree, and anchored the swing.

We had endless hours of fun challenging each other to see who could swing the highest as our shoe tips reached for the tiny tree which, all these seventy-three years later, now looms over the front steps and that narrow cement path.

Agnes and I spent endless hours playing with Alexander, rolling the ball back and forth to him on that narrow concrete path, and watching how he fussed over his shiny red and green metal truck. Alexander and Agnes were both sickly children. Alexander had Rheumatic Fever when he was an infant and was predisposed to colds and bouts with the flu.

Each morning without fail, Mom gave Alexander and Agnes a glass of orange juice with a teaspoon of cod liver oil. A memory that has never left me is of Agnes and Alexander and the funniest faces they made swallowing down their cod liver oil while reaching for their glasses of orange juice.

People did a lot of walking in those years, including our family because Dad rarely drove his pea-green colored 1926 Essex with a black leatherette top because it was only used for emergencies. Mom never learned how to drive, and there weren't any buses yet running from our area into Englewood. And so, we were told: "The walk will do us good."

One morning, our Mother needed to pick up a pair of new glasses from the optometrist whose office was near Dean and Engle Streets in Englewood. I was put in charge of looking after Agnes and Alexander and waited with them in front of a little tea room frequented by local business people. We stood at the window watching a couple sitting at a table as their waitress came with two deep bowls of berries, perhaps blackberries or strawberries, and their cups of tea.

My sister and I always took note of something unusual or different and whenever we did, we would go home and imitate what we had seen. That afternoon was no different. We went to the brink of the woods, picked our blackberries and elderberries and made believe we were sitting in the tea room being served our goblets of berries as we had seen that morning.

When blueberries were in season, at ten cents a box, our Mother always bought several boxes, and promptly put us to the task of helping her make the jam. Agnes and I removed the tiny stems while she boiled glass jars to bottle the jam for the winter months. During May and June, we had our fill of all the strawberries we could pick from the briars next to our home.

Before it became too cold to play outside, Agnes and I would pretend that we were housekeepers; Agnes was Mrs. Treer and I was Mrs. Grape. A good imagination could carry one a long way when there weren't any toys available. Our grocery store was the woods where we "shopped," looking at the leaves and small plants as though they were vegetables. One of our very "useful" plants was skunk cabbage. We'd take a butter knife out into the yard and use it to cut the "ham slice" or a "piece of steak" from a great big cabbage leaf. Sometimes a stone would represent a bone, or a potato. And the berries--well, black berries and strawberries didn't need any substitution, and served as our "snacks" until dinner time.

I turned nine years old that October, and a few weeks later on October 25, 1931, the George Washington Bridge opened which, for a nine year old, was not nearly as important as ghosts and goblins on Halloween a week later.

Agnes began to miss a considerable amount of time from school with recurring colds and sore throat episodes as winter began. Then, suddenly, she was taken to Holy Name Hospital in Teaneck where she was diagnosed with Pneumonia. The doctor explained that children suffering recurring colds and throat illnesses did much better when their tonsils were removed. Routinely, it was a three-day stay for the patient who checked in on a Friday afternoon for the procedure, recuperated Saturday, and was released to go home on Sunday afternoon.

And so, on a late Saturday afternoon following the removal of Agnes' tonsils, we all walked to the hospital to see her. Mom stayed on with Agnes, and Dad, Alexander and I went to catch the bus for home. We walked part of the way from the bus stop when Dad realized I was lagging behind. He was carrying little Alexander, came back to me, and took my hand. "Let's see who can walk the fastest," he said. Of course, he really had slowed his pace, although I didn't realize it at the time. I remember him humming his favorite song, *Life is Just a Bowl of Cherries*. In later years, he added, "But we can do without the pits?"

Agnes came home the next day to find a new doll waiting for her. We all shared our happy words for her recovery. And, you may find this a bit unusual, but the doctor came to our home several times to check on the progress Agnes was making. She was so proud that she had gone through the surgery and had stayed alone in the hospital.

As the eight o'clock hour approached, she curled up in the oversized stuffed chair in the living room to listen to Eddie Cantor, *Banjo Eyes*, as he was known following his appearances in Ziegfeld's Follies. He opened his Sunday evening broadcast with *"I Love to Spend This Sunday With You..."* He was Agnes' favorite entertainer; at seven years old, she never missed listening to his Sunday night show sponsored by the Chase and Sanborn Coffee Company. On Monday and Tuesday, Agnes reprised Eddie Cantor's theme song for us, singing the words as naturally as if she'd been singing the song for years.

The anticipation of Sunday night with Eddie Cantor always carried the expectation of a "special treat." It began on Friday when the Duggan bread man, an Irishman who looked very much like the Irish actor Pat O'Brien, drove his horse-drawn wagon down Manhattan Avenue. Every Friday afternoon, Mom would buy her loaf of whole wheat bread, rolls, or raisin bread. They enjoyed talking about Ireland and their relatives back home. The *special treat* was a chocolate layer cake that we viewed on Saturday and enjoyed on Sunday while listening to Eddie Cantor. Needless to say, every time I see a chocolate layer cake, I think of those Sunday evenings with the family and Eddie Cantor all those seventy-four years ago.

Agnes never tired of playing with her dolls and doll carriage. She was always fussing over them when she wasn't playing with Alexander. She had a little tea set and we would pour our "tea" pretending our version of "high tone" talk, just as the actors had done on the radio programs we heard.

While Agnes was a very dainty little person, I wasn't. I liked brooms and things with which I could be active and accomplish something. Mom always made a point of mentioning to friends that all I wanted was a wheel barrel, a rake, and a shovel (child size) because I liked to do yard work. I never asked, but I think she was indirectly saying that I was grown-up for my age. However, she also could have been suggesting that I wasn't anything like Agnes.

Another horse-drawn wagon that came into the neighborhood three times a year was driven by the little Italian *Rag Man* ringing his bell and announcing his arrival: "Rags...Rags!" Frugality was the order of the day. We saved the clothes we had outgrown or that had become unwearable. He also paid for newspapers that he subsequently sold to be recycled. And Agnes and I would race for our saved bundle of rags and batch of newspapers.

The *Rag Man* paid as much as fifteen to twenty-five cents for a bundle of rags. Back then, a dollar had buying power so, getting paid for a bundle of rags gave Agnes and me spending money for a long while.

The milkman was another who, during the 1930s, came in a horse-drawn wagon. He'd pick up our empty glass milk bottles and leave fresh ones in the wooden milk box. Later, in the mid-1930s, heavily-waxed light cardboard containers were introduced and available in stores.

Just before Christmas, Mom would always hide candy and nuts high up on a shelf at the very back of a kitchen cabinet. She'd fill a new pair of long brown stockings (which we'd later wear to school) with the candy and nuts and then, slide the brown stockings into our decorated Christmas stockings that hung from a shelf on the bookcase in the living room. She was so practical.

I remember our helping Mom on Saturday mornings and washing all those pairs of brown stockings, hanging them out to dry, and then ironing them. The hand-washing was done on a washboard in a stone wash tub; (the luxury of a washing machine came later, in 1938). The clothes were soaped well with *The Gold Dust Twins Soap Powder,* a bright orange box with two black images on the container. Believe it or not, we actually enjoyed doing the laundry, especially in wintertime because, if it was cold enough, the clothes would freeze on the line. Alexander, Agnes and I would laugh hysterically when the clothes came off the line, particularly Dad's trousers and long-sleeved shirts, which came in frozen stiff-as-a-board.

Pack Up Your Troubles in Your Old Kit Bag was a happy tune back then; if only it had been that easy...

1932

I think the worst year of the Depression was 1932. Unemployment was reported at 24.1%. A postage stamp was only two cents, but was increased to three cents by mid year. And the League of Nations (the U.N.'s forerunner) was attempting to bring the Republic of China and Japan together for peace negotiations. In November, President Hoover was singing, *Say It Isn't So,* when Franklin Delano Roosevelt won the presidential election.

All that we heard on the radio and all that we had read in the newspapers was about ever increasing numbers of unemployed people and how desperate they were. Thousands of mortgages had been foreclosed--including some of our neighbors who, mercifully, were able to hold onto their homes because the banks didn't have the resources to take back everyone's home-- then sit with them until, and IF, a buyer came along.

The government constantly put their own *spin* on the state of the nation, telling everybody that *"things are getting better."* And the people asked: *"Getting better for who?"* Men and women were walking the streets, desperately looking for work--any kind of work, or standing in *bread lines* or *soup kitchens*. There were reports of people around the country living like hobos in shanty towns, called *Hoovervilles*, named for President Herbert Hoover who was blamed for the stock market crash and the Depression which ensued.

People traveled to other parts of the state and throughout the country for whatever jobs were being offered. Success seemed to have evaporated while poverty came packaged with illness and broken homes. We, like few others we knew, were fortunate to have had our primary wage-earner still employed. Dad was one of the fortunate ones, even though Mom was fond of saying, "If yer bosses continue to reduce yer weekly paycheck, ye'll be payin' them just to be able to go to work!" Complaining or disputing the continuing pay reductions was not something anyone dared do with management. Teachers' pay was continually lowered, until they were laid off because there wasn't enough tax money in the county coffers.

Dad was earning thirty-one dollars a week in 1932. It seems incomprehensible today to think that a family of five could survive on thirty-one dollars a week. We nearly didn't. But, the reality was that the dollar was backed by gold and *worth* a whole one-hundred pennies. Our dollar is no longer backed by gold.

How strange and surprising is the remembering of a long-forgotten memory tucked away in the recesses of our minds. It was a day when Agnes, Alexander, and I went shopping with our Mother...

We always went into Englewood to shop at the Atlantic & Pacific Tea Company's grocery store which everybody shortened to the A & P. I can still see the iron cash register on the counter and the rows of canned food on shelves behind that counter.

Shopping in grocery stores was not as it is today. We ordered everything through the counter clerk; a two-pound wedge of sharp American cheese was cut from the block of cheese the clerk lifted from a barrel, then it was weighed. Cans of stewed tomatoes were lifted from the top shelf with the help of a long pole with metal prongs at the end which grabbed hold of the cans, one at a time. Tub butter was kept in a refrigerator case for which the clerk would rip off a long sheet of brown parchment-type wrapping paper; the clerk would then set the chunk of butter in the center of the paper, draw-up the edges and tie a cord around the gathered ends of the paper. It was how a shopper's purchases were carried home before paper grocery bags came into vogue. The cheese, stewed tomatoes, tub butter, two boxes of Mueller's round macaroni, a loaf of bread, five pounds of potatoes, two cans of evaporated milk, and a smoked ham shoulder usually totaled about five dollars.

Mom's favorite Icy Point Salmon could be bought for ten cents a can. A five-pound bag of sugar was twenty-five cents. A loaf of bread was ten cents, a dozen eggs only fifteen cents; and a wax carton of milk could be bought for ten cents. A very good steak sold for twelve to fifteen cents per pound. (In addition to the fact that today's dollar is no longer worth one-hundred pennies, I wonder who we should thank for all the antibiotics and hormones which, certainly, have added to the costs?)

Mom grew our string beans, tomatoes, rhubarb (usually for a pie), baked her special recipe for potato bread, and often made her famous

"Shepard's Pie" with ten-cent-a-pound ground beef that the butcher freshly ground for her.

Mom would buy baby chicks from a chicken farm northwest of Englewood and keep them in a box under the warmth of a light bulb. I remember how Agnes sat for hours watching those chicks, gently patting their little furry heads. Our Dad built a wire coop for them where they grew to full size, eventually becoming a roasted chicken dinner which was a typical dinner of the times. Recalling that little wire coop makes me remember a neighbor's two roosters whose crowing faithfully announced daybreak on Manhattan Avenue.

During our early years in the house, we had what was called *Congoleum*, an oil cloth linoleum designed to look like a fine Persian rug, that covered the hardwood floors. Magazines of the 1920s and 30s had advertised Congoleum that could be mopped and waxed and, depending upon the size of the room, would cost from six to twelve dollars. Then Agnes and I came home from school one afternoon and stepped onto a beautiful wool rug in our living room. As I recall, my sister and I spent many happy hours playing and sitting on that lovely wool rug.

Chenille spreads came into vogue during the mid- to late 1930s, and ranged in price from about two to four dollars. Clothing was made of cotton, rayon, or silk. Wool was used primarily in coats, along with imitation fur on the collars and cuffs for the average folks.

New York City's WOR-Radio host, John B. Gambling, continued to open his six a.m. morning shows with the song: *"Look for the silver lining, somewhere the sun is shining..."* I always associate this song with Dad leaving for work early each morning, and Agnes and I leaving for our walk to St. Cecilia's School.

Rudy Vallee sang *Goodnight, Sweetheart* and Wayne King, The Waltz King, sang *Dream a Little Dream of Me*. One has only to hear a few lyrics of a song to be magically transported back in time. Even the chill in the air has a way of nudging the reminiscence of a day, or just a moment in time, like the gray chilly day Agnes, Alexander, and I walked with Mom to the butcher shop just a few doors north of the Plaza Theater on Van Brunt Street. Furry gray and brown rabbits hung on hooks from a shiny chrome bar in the butcher shop window above sliced lamb chops and steaks displayed on crushed ice.

We stood shivering in the cold shop as Mom told the butcher what she wanted. He had a time understanding her Irish brogue and, being the precocious child that I was, I sternly told the man, "Don't you understand English?" My Mother wants four lamb chops!" Mom leaned down to me and softly said, "It's good to be speakin' up for yer'self, Margaret... but, don't ye be soundin' so brash and so bold."

I took my reprimand in silence while Agnes and Alexander pranced through the sawdust on the floor. It was all well and good for Mom to say I was brash and bold--but God help anyone who *really* got on the wrong side of Mom!

Some towns seem to be blessed with "do-gooders" ... you know, the kind; those who position themselves to do good for *others* they judge as "inferior or needy." I remember a wintery day when one such woman came into our neighborhood trying to "do good" with several pairs of *used* shoes that nobody seemed to want. The woman introduced herself as a member of some local women's club while unbuttoning her fur coat. She lifted Agnes and her doll onto her lap and tossed a pair of saddle shoes onto the floor in front of me.

To say that Mom was indignant and highly insulted by this "hoy-falloy" would be a gross understatement. "My daughters have shoes," our Mother said, lifting the shoes off the floor.

The woman straightened the fur collar around her neck and said, "I want to do something to her advantage."

Mom walked across the room and leveled her blue eyes on the woman whose only objective was to "feel good" about herself. "Ye'll take these shoes and leave--or, ye'll be leavin' with them gracing yer neck, along with that dead animal yer wearin'. Now, get out of my home!"

She never understood the need in some who carried themselves with such arrogance and haughty superiority. When Dad came home later that evening, the event was relived--and Mom was furious all over again. "Just because there are those of us who don't live in those fancy Victorian houses, which are mortgaged to the roof, I might add, while our home is paid for and we don't go around wearing dead animals to impress anyone, I'll not be put upon or insulted by the likes of them!"

In February, our Mother had even more to say about Pope Pius XI's meeting with the Italian Fascist dictator, Benito Mussolini, who actually had stepped inside the venerable walls of the Vatican. She did not approve, even if the Pope had given the dictator the opportunity to save his sinful soul. Neither Agnes nor I understood her blustery reproach of the man who had met the Pope in Italy; that is, not until much later.

Englewood had its quaint, hometown charm, as well as its shoppes which offered something for everyone. O'Malley's was the little store that held the most curiosity for Agnes and me. It sat on the opposite side of Demarest Avenue, across from St. Cecelia's Church and the school. We were two little girls, only eight and ten years old, yet we felt so grown-up with the few pennies in our pockets and our own decisions to make.

When school let out, Agnes and I always made a last visit to church before going home. But this day, Agnes and I looked at our three pennies allowance that we had saved all week long, then looked across the street to the two-story Victorian home that had been built in the 1890s, with its little stoop that led up to O'Malley's Candy Store.

We walked down Demarest Avenue in front of St. Cecelia's to the corner at Waldo Place. I took hold of Agnes' hand, carefully looking both ways, then crossed Demarest Avenue. We walked up to O'Malley's window. We stood in our wool coats and caps, rosy cheeks, runny noses, and our pennies. I walked up the little stoop, and the tingle of the bell over the door announced our arrival. A lady came from behind the draped doorway at the rear of the shop.

We walked to the glass counter, searching the array of candies and knowing that a *MaryJane* candy bar was only a penny. I said, "My sister and I will have two MaryJane candies, please." It's a special memory for no other reason but that it was a decision we had made on our own and which we carried out in a very grown-up way.

Going to O'Malley's became a weekly treat for us and later, when our allowance was increased to five cents, we tried a *Mellow Roll,* made of vanilla ice cream with chocolate crackers, something akin to the ice cream sandwich of today, but in a different shape.

Mother took Alexander, Agnes, and me to our very first movie one Saturday afternoon at the Plaza Theater to see *The Kid From Spain* with Eddie Cantor. I vaguely recall, it was a comedy and very difficult to follow for little people like us, only five, eight and ten years old. Agnes couldn't believe her eyes. She was actually seeing the man she had faithfully listened to every Sunday night on the radio. (She talked about it for weeks after, as well as singing his radio theme song.)

I clearly remember the beginning days of March 1932...

Mom had taken all of her dishes and glasses out of the china cabinet and then moved it to the center of the floor where other things from the living room were standing. She was going to wallpaper not only the dining room, but the living room as well. She took down the picture of Father McCormick, the priest who had performed their wedding, and removed it from the frame. I don't know why, except that perhaps she wasn't going to hang his picture on the wall again.

On one of the living room walls hung an almost life-sized, black-and-white chalk portrait of Dad's father, Alexander Griffin. I remember he had a mustache. I tried to avoid looking at the portrait as it hung on the wall because I didn't like the ghostly feeling it gave me. (I didn't mind *The Shadow* or *The Witch's Tale* because I was in control of my own visualizations.) Thankfully, Mom had taken Grandpa Griffin's portrait off the wall and pulled it from the frame, as well.

Agnes picked up the picture of Grandpa Griffin and proceeded to chase me throughout the house, out the front door, and down the steps outside, and all along the cement path beside the house. She laughed hysterically, thrusting that picture up in my face each time I turned my head. She had such great fun until Mom finally put a stop to it. From that time forward, I have never liked huge portraits. The eeriness of that portrait somehow defined for me the shock and sadness of the news broadcasts that began the next day...

The twenty-month-old son of America's Aviator, Colonel Charles A. Lindbergh and his wife, Anne Morrow Lindbergh, had been kidnapped from his crib in his nursery on the second floor of their Hopewell, New Jersey home. Agnes cut out of every newspaper and magazine all the photographs she could find of little Charles Augustas Lindbergh III, then pasted them onto the pages in a scrapbook. The scrapbook that I look at today brings back so many memories of that long ago time. The print is a little faded and the glue has since dried and given up its hold on the articles and pictures Agnes meticulously cut and pasted into her keepsake book. It certainly is putting my hands on yesterday as I review the past.

The newspapers were filled with articles and photos of their beautiful baby boy with his curly locks, sitting in a little lawn chair. Information *Wanted* posters with photographs and description: *Age, twenty months. Hair, blond, curly. Weight, 27 to 30 lbs. Eyes, dark blue. Height, 29 inches. Complexion, light. Deep dimple in center of chin; dressed in one-piece coverall night suit,"* were seen everywhere for months later. (The Superintendent of the New Jersey State Police, Colonel H. Norman Schwarzkopf, was the official in charge. Yes, he was the father of General "Stormin" Norman Schwarzkopf who had directed the first war offensive against Saddam Hussein in Iraq in 1991.)

The kidnapping of the Lindbergh baby brought forth a rage among the citizenry who were wholly incapable of conceiving that such a despicable act had been committed not only against America's hero, but against an innocent baby. The kidnapper wanted fifty-thousand dollars for the baby's return.

Dad told us that Mrs. Lindbergh's father, Ambassador Dwight Morrow, had lived on an estate in a prestigious neighborhood on the Englewood Cliffs of the Palisades. Reporters back then were no different than they are today and camped out at the Lindbergh estate hoping to see either Anne Morrow Lindbergh, Colonel Lindbergh or, perhaps, they just might get lucky and *get a scoop* about the kidnapping.

John B. Gambling gave updates on the crime, and the country prayed for the baby's safe return, as we did during our bedtime prayers. The Lindbergh baby was only a few years younger than Alexander; thus, his safe return meant even more to us.

In early May, the remains of little Charles Augustas Lindbergh III were found near the Lindbergh home in Hopewell.

As the Depression grew worse, unrest among the populace intensified when fifteen-thousand World War I veterans marched on the nation's capitol. They were called the *Bonus Marchers*--men who had fought during World War I and who only wanted the bonuses that had been promised them. The Senate, again, denied them with their veto vote against payment of the bonuses. The Army's Calvary, headed by Dwight D. Eisenhower, Douglas MacArthur, and George Patton, lobbed tear gas canisters into the Veterans' tents which had been set-up across the Potomac River. Several Veterans had been shot, as well.

The politicians had chosen to ignore its country's veterans while diligently looking for innovative ways to grow their own power and omnipotence. We were in the worst condition this country had ever experienced (short of war), and what did the *fat cats* in Washington do? They approved a *gas tax* of one-cent per gallon.

Thousands of Americans lost their homes and were living in shanty towns. Thousands more of children had been prevented from going to school because the schools had been closed. Hundreds of thousands of people couldn't afford to buy food, much less pay for gasoline... the Revenue Act of 1932 was a *tax* decreed by politicians who had found yet *another way* to seize the People's money--even if collecting that extra penny tax had to wait until after the *Great* Depression.

In November, Franklin Delano Roosevelt defeated Herbert Hoover, while German president Hindenburg negotiated with Hitler about forming a *new* government.

Before the year's end, Mom asked me if I still wanted a wheel barrel, a rake, and a shovel for Christmas. Of course, I did! I loved doing yard work and, oh how I loved to rake the leaves in the Fall. (I also knew it would mean a few more pennies in my weekly allowance!) Agnes, on the other hand, wanted another doll to add to her collection so she could fuss with them when she wasn't playing with Alexander. I do believe that Agnes finally gave in to me and we put her dolls in my wheel barrel and took them for a ride on that little cement path covered with snow that Christmas Day.

Three days later, five-year-old Alexander became ill with what the doctors thought was a case of the flu, and admitted him to Holy Name Hospital in Teaneck. Tests confirmed that Alexander had Scarlet Fever, the highly contagious and feared disease. Dad was instructed to immediately remove Alexander's bed clothes, sheets, window curtains, and even his mattress. We were told not to go into his room until everything--even the walls--had been washed with a special disinfectant solution.

Two days later, we learned that the doctors had moved Alexander to the contagion ward at Bergen Pines, the county hospital in Paramus. Dad cranked up his 1926 Essex and drove us to Bergen Pines.

I remember the huge hospital complex as we followed our parents through the hospital doors, only to be stopped. Children weren't allowed in the hospital and so, Dad told us to sit and wait in the lobby until he returned, just as Alexander and I had done when Agnes was in the hospital.

He paused to talk with a nurse, then returned and told us to follow the nurse outside. She guided us to a window at Alexander's room so we could see him. I remember Alexander lying on the crib bed and looking up at out parents. Dad pointed toward us at the window, but Alexander was too weak to turn his head, even when Agnes tapped on the window. "You'll be home soon, Alexander," she said, waving her little hands and smiling at him.

1933

The spirit of the holidays evaporated. The doctors told us that Alexander was also fighting Pneumonia. We sat in the lobby while our parents went to be with our brother. I thought of what Mom had told me when I asked her about the strange garlands I'd seen on the doors of houses when we walked to the hospital with her. Some of the wreaths had purple and black ribbons, which I thought strange for celebrating the Christmas holidays. Mom explained that a purple or black ribbon meant that a grown-up had died; a white ribbon tied to a wreath meant a child had died.

At eight-thirty in the morning on January 3, 1933, a policeman came to our home with word that Alexander had died.

The undertaker from Conklin's Funeral Home had driven to Bergen Pines and placed Alexander's body into a metallic-sealed casket that went inside a wooden coffin. Board of Health regulations required the sealing of a casket for those who had died of any contagious disease.

My memories of that day at the cemetery are as clear to me now as if I were standing there beside Agnes, watching two workers lifting Alexander's casket, and starting down the winding path to the grave site. Our priest came to the cemetery to bless the coffin and to say a few prayers over Alexander while Agnes and I stood silent in the blinding sunlight that bitterly cold day at Mt. Carmel Cemetery, just off

Engle Street in Tenafly. We were two little girls shedding uncertain tears of what was happening as we watched our parents crying over Alexander's grave.

I still have the *feel* of shivering as Agnes and I stood numb with fright and hurt-filled hearts. The feelings and images remain, as does the vision of Agnes at that particular hour on that day, her little finger at her lip, crying tears that would not stop, even as we walked back over the little railroad bridge to Dean Street.

Alexander's passing had been a cruel reality. Our Mother tried to comfort us by telling us that Alexander was in Heaven and there would be no more pain and suffering for him. She believed her words, there was no doubt in our minds. And, as hard as Agnes and I tried to be brave about Alexander's going to Heaven, we always found ourselves in his room, by his iron bed, and Mom would come in, pull her embroidered cotton handkerchief from her apron pocket and daub our endless tears.

It was a cold, gray time of winter days and nights filled with sadness that rejected retreat. Mom had lost so much weight by the end of February that her dresses, which usually hung to the calves of her legs, now touched the tops of her shoes.

Our Mother kept us home from school one wintery March day and announced that we were going into the city. Father Dolan, our priest at St. Cecelia's had given her mission. We held tightly to her hands as she boarded us on the Third Avenue trolley that took us to Bronx. She walked us across the Boston Post Road and I can see us ducking into the alcoves of stores to get out of the cutting winds. Our destination was Benziger Brothers Publishers for a copy of *In Heaven We Know Our Own,* written in 1863 by Father Rene Blot, a French priest. It was *Solace for the Suffering,* as noted in its subtitle and which Father Dolan had strongly recommended the family read.

Sorrow replaced worry, and fear no longer occupied our parents' thoughts. Life was a day-to-day existence, and though the radio continued to bring us the music of the time and the usual shows we had been accustomed to hearing, nothing was the same--except the *Great* Depression. The *"Great Anguish"* continued at its hellish pace, with unemployment reported at 25.2%.

Erskine Caldwell's *Tobacco Road* was published that year which, years later, I thought had only served to deepen the country's psychological depression. Prohibition ended that February, and the government outlawed marijuana. (And, we've seen how successful the government's been with that!)

It was also in March when everyone heard Roosevelt's inauguration speech in which he referenced the *Great* Depression with his famous quote: "We have nothing to fear, but fear itself."

Dad looked at Mom and said: "He ought to tell that to the people who are in fear of losing their homes and those who are starving!" The day after his inauguration, FDR ordered a "bank holiday." (Which certainly didn't ease the people's fear!) Panic seized the people who *feared* they wouldn't be able to withdraw what little money they had. Our parents didn't have a bank account; instead, they had purchased a few Post Office certificates that were guaranteed by the government and, as Dad had said, "At least we know the government isn't going out of business anytime soon!"

Roosevelt wasted no time instituting his *New Deal,* beginning with The Tennessee Valley Authority, the Federal Securities Act, and the Civil Works Administration. But, to make matters worse, he took our currency off of the gold standard. (The people's 'fear' moved to full-blown anger!)

Radio Station WOR continued broadcasting the music of the day: *Build A Little Home ... Gotta Get Up And Go To Work ...* and *We're In The Money* -- all of which made *The Boulevard of Broken Dreams* the only truthful reality put to music that year.

The Golddiggers of 1933 was a hit and Dad joked, "What a great way to commemorate our worthless money!" Dad had a wonderful sense of humor that lifted Mom's spirits and ours.

Just before year's end, our parents contracted for a second level on the house with two extra rooms and an updated kitchen and a laundry room. The second floor was extended over the two new rooms below and became a third bedroom. Agnes and I pretended to "skate" (in our sox) across the "new" wide-planked wood floors that came from a home in Englewood, built in the 1860s. The warm pine flooring, though slated to be destroyed and thrown away, became "new" floors for us. Practicality was the order of the day and, of course, Mr. Wurm came to help Dad put the pine wood flooring down.

I remember there was also great concern that we might not be able to find a staircase that would match the pine flooring. Dad knew someone who had learned that Englewood's First Free School, built sometime around the early 1870s on Englewood Avenue, had a staircase--but, the school was going to be torn down.

Dad quickly arranged with the wrecker to deliver the staircase that was installed in the house. Although the steps were much wider than the staircase steps in houses, it fit beautifully. More importantly was the fact that the stairs came from a building nearly the same age as our house. That solid oak, hundred-plus year-old staircase is still in the old house today. I often wondered how many little feet climbed up and down that staircase before it came to us.

1934

When I think back to 1934, I recall that it was the year of the criminal. Bonnie Parker and Clyde Barrow entered the history books after shooting two police officers in Texas. A month later, both were killed during a police manhunt. I saw the 1967 movie with Warren Beatty and Faye Dunaway and thought then how accurately it reflected the attitude of the people during the Thirties.

I especially remember the nighttime scene of the little motel bungalow (where Bonnie and Clyde were staying), Eddie Cantor's voice drifting in the still of the night, and the sound of a car's wheels rolling over the gravel drive, all of which captured the ambiance of the times.

One very strong recollection about the two bank robbers is that they were quoted as saying of the bankers: "They took from us, now we're taking from them." The People knew that Bonnie and Clyde had used guns to steal from the bankers; but then, the People hadn't elect Bonnie Parker and Clyde Barrow as they had their elected representatives who had used pens while a 22% unemployment rate gripped the country.

John Dillinger had a twenty-five-thousand-dollar bounty on his head which probably had something to do with his being shot to death outside of a movie house in Chicago; he had just seen *Public Enemy No. 1*. Baby Face Nelson also went to his "bank in the sky." It was also the year that the Austrian paper hanger, Adolf Hitler, became Germany's Chancellor and Fuhrer.

Clark Gable starred in *It Happened One Night.* And that year, Agnes and I fell in love with little Shirley Temple and all of her movies... *Stand Up and Cheer, Little Miss Marker, Baby Take A Bow, Bright Eyes,* and *Now and Forever.*

In Canada, the Dionne Quintuplets were born, starting another craze with little girls who wanted the set of composition dolls. I don't recall if Agnes had the Dionne Quintuplet dolls; it's hard to imagine that any doll could have taken the place of Shirley Temple with Agnes.

If you're wondering why I keep speaking of the movies well, seventy years ago, an afternoon or evening at the movie house was a special event. Remember, back then television was not available to the masses. Believe it or not, newspapers provided entertainment, especially the sections that featured the movie stars. Newspapers were the primary source for news events, and for political, social and business affairs.

There were no videos or DVDs; no computers or computer games. It was either listening to the radio, the 78 rpm records, or the movie theaters for those who could spare the price of admission.

Everyone dressed-up in their best attire which, for ladies also included hats and gloves. Men wore dress slacks and a jacket, or a suit with a shirt and tie. Their hair was neatly combed and their shoes were always shined.

Stopping at a local restaurant or soda fountain after the show was the thing to do if one had a few extra pennies in their pocket and wanted to make an afternoon or evening *extra special*.

Shortly after the house renovation was completed, I remember starting up our "new" staircase one afternoon and caught sight of Agnes. She was taking great care in positioning all of her dolls on the landing to the raised level where the third bedroom had been added. She didn't see me as she slowly began pacing back and forth in front of them singing, *I Only Have Eyes For You.* I thought it was a little silly, but she did have a pleasant voice and really was cute to watch, though I never told her then.

Agnes also had a little kitten...

After Little Flower devotions one Tuesday evening at church, our family stopped by Moe Lieberman's store and purchased some Hershey candy bars. We noticed Agnes meticulously wrapping up a little piece of her candy bar and tucking it inside her coat pocket. "I'm saving it for my kitten," she said, her laughing blue eyes wide in anticipation of giving the chocolate to her kitten.

Well, sad to say, the little kitten was behind the French doors in the living room that I quickly opened--hitting the kitten in the head. The poor little thing never had the piece of candy Agnes painstakingly wrapped and saved for him.

Mom wasn't pleased, and Agnes was in dreadful tears as Dad lifted the little ball of fur, took it outside, and buried it behind the house.

It was a very sad event made even worse when Mom said I was "too fast, too clumsy, and entirely too careless." It wasn't a pleasant evening for me at all. Agnes stayed mad at me for all of the next day!

Sunday mornings continued as every other Sunday had... we walked to Englewood for the eight o'clock morning mass and after, we stopped into Moe Lieberman's for our Sunday newspapers. When we got home, Mom put on a pot of coffee and Agnes and I set the table while Mom prepared the bacon and eggs, never failing to ask us how we liked our eggs cooked. Dad drank his coffee and Mom, Agnes, and I sipped our tea.

Sometimes, on warm summer days after church, we all would walk the "Seven Sisters," the series of hills from Englewood to the Palisades along the Hudson River. We spent hours watching the ships sailing up and down, wondering what a boat ride would be like.

On one of those afternoons, our Dad told us about a very sad tragedy he had witnessed along New York's East River. It happened in 1904 when he was fourteen years old. The *General Slocum,* a sidewheel steamship, named for the Civil War soldier and New York Congressman, Henry W. Slocum, took passengers on sightseeing excursions around New York City. A church group of nearly thirteen-hundred people from the German district of Little Germany in Manhattan had chartered the boat to sail the East River for their day-long celebration.

A fire started in the ship and, as Dad told the story, nearly a thousand passengers, mostly women and children, had either burned to death or drowned. The life preservers were old and rotting and couldn't keep the children afloat. The heavy-skirted clothes the women wore only weighted them down, making any attempt to swim impossible. Our Dad had said that when he reached North Brother Island, off the Bronx shore, the sight was one he said he'd never forget.

I remember how Agnes had cried, staring down at the river and saying: "We should always say a prayer for those poor souls when we come here." And, she always did, each time we reached the Palisades.

If you were *somebody* who wanted to be *noticed* in Englewood, you had to *be seen* on a summer afternoon in Baumgarten's Ice Cream Parlor. There was also Stelling's Ice Cream Parlor, the place Englewood's young people mostly frequented after football games and such. Agnes and I were too young in 1934 and not in the least interested in anyone except Shirley Temple, *The Shadow*, and Eddie Cantor.

Sam Dincin's Drugstore had an old-fashioned charm with two show globes, one with red-colored water and one with blue-colored water, that hung from the ceiling on either side of the front door in the two show windows. Down from Dincin's was the Hecht's Department Store, which I mention because of a memory I have of our Dad stopping into Dincin's to have a prescription filled. We all sat in the car, freezing and looking at the store windows when we noticed a sign in the Hecht's window that read: *Half-Priced Bathing Suits.* Agnes and I laughed, joking that no one would want to buy a bathing suit in the dead of winter. Our Mother explained that while it may be wintertime, buying a half-priced bathing suit for the summer was *being frugal.* "If yer going to survive in this world, ye had better know there are plenty of ways to spend money; it's the knowin' how to save yer money that will keep ye out of the poor house."

On Columbus Day 1934, October 12 to be exact, Rommy came to visit and have dinner with us because his wife had died a few weeks earlier. To everyone's surprise, he brought boxes filled with his wife's clothes, mostly in the turn-of-the-century style that she so loved and some of which still had their price tags. There were also toys and dolls his children had played with when they were young. I can see that afternoon so clearly...

Rommy was sitting with our parents around the kitchen table having coffee and tea when we heard a ripping sound. We all went to the living room and saw Agnes pulling at a flap on one of the boxes and struggling to lift the dresses out. She walked between us and into the kitchen, to one of the cabinet drawers, and removed the bottle of brown-colored mucilage we used as glue. Then, obviously with a purpose, she began de-tangling the ribbons from among the dresses she had already taken out.

She coated the ribbons with glue, carefully placing them as decoration on the sides of the empty box. She searched through the dresses, pulled one out, along with a pair of mid-heeled shoes, walked out onto the sun porch and closed the sheer-draped French doors behind her.

We all walked back into the kitchen while Mom checked on the dinner. A little while later, Agnes reappeared wearing one of Mrs. Rhome's dresses. Although Agnes was only ten years old, she was clever enough to have tied a ribbon around her tiny waist to hold up the bulk of the skirting so she wouldn't trip. She also wore a broad-brimmed hat and was wobbling on Mrs. Rhome's mid-heeled shoes while struggling to hold several of the newly-arrived dolls in her arms.

Dad had surmised what Agnes was up to and carried Alexander's stroller and her decorated box out the front door and to the yard. We all went to the windows on the sun porch and watched Agnes as she set the decorated box on top of Alexander's stroller, filling it with her "new" dolls, and proceeded down the cement path beside the house, pushing her dolls, and singing *The Object of My Affection.*

Agnes was far more determined and adventuresome than I. If she wasn't asking to walk the Palisades to look at the ships passing on the Hudson, she was asking Dad to take her "flying."

There was a German couple with two grown sons living a block behind us on Washington Place. One of the sons had been a flyer in the

German air corps during World War I and, though I don't recall where he had gotten the biplane he kept on their property, Agnes had seen it one day while walking with Dad.

From the moment she spotted that old plane, there wasn't a week that went by that Agnes hadn't asked Dad to take her to the neighbors so she could "fly" the plane. The German couple were very friendly and always stopped Dad to talk whenever they saw him. Their son had noticed how infatuated Agnes was with his plane and told Dad that she was welcome to sit in it.

On their way home from each walk, she always said the same thing: "I want to fly high up into the clouds!" Having seen *Bright Eyes* with Shirley Temple, and having seen little Shirley "flying" her *Good Ship Lollipop* airplane, there was no doubt in anyone's mind that Agnes felt if flying was okay for Shirley Temple, it was certainly good enough for her. Dad got such a kick out of seeing Agnes sitting in that old plane that he could never refuse her.

In November, there was a raffle at school and we wound up with tickets to a matinee. It was (of course) Shirley Temple in *Now & Forever* with Gary Cooper, who played Shirley's widower father, and Carole Lombard who, naturally, fell in love with Gary Cooper and Shirley.

November 11--Armistice Day--was a particularly ritualistic event because everyone, no matter where they stood, stopped in their tracks to remember those who had lost their lives during World War I. Wherever you were at eleven minutes after eleven o'clock on the eleventh day of the eleventh month, you froze in your tracks to show your respect for those lost souls.

We understood the reason for the solemnness of the day from Dad's many hours of history lessons. He and Mom, too, had told us about the thousands of soldiers and nurses who had boarded ships in the harbor, laying down life and limb to help those fighting throughout Europe.

I have to admit that it does infuriate me when I think of the ingratitude Europeans have for the thousands of Americans who sacrificed their lives for the very freedoms Europeans enjoy today.

1934 was the year I remember Agnes and I listening to the new radio program *The Make Believe Ballroom* which was broadcast on New York's WNEW. The show was hosted by Martin Block who played the music of the dance bands. Of all the words of advice we heard as children growing up, we always remembered Martin Block's:

"A thought for all my young listeners: if you have an opportunity to experience going some place special--a place you really want to see, or enjoy a special occasion... do it now. See as much as you can because you'll never see through the eyes of a forty-year-old what you would have seen through the eyes of a twenty-year-old."

1935

Unemployment was reported at 20.1% and Parker Brothers thought the people would like to own *Park Place* and *The Boardwalk*, perhaps, even railroads with their new game of *Monopoly*. It seemed appropriate after hearing George and Ira Gershwin's *Porgy & Bess* tune, *I Got Plenty O' Nuttin' ... And nuttin's plenty for me!* which probably had millions of destitute Americans believing that the *Rich* must have had a *monopoly* on the good life.

January had just settled in when Ma Barker and her gang were killed in a shootout with the F.B.I. Our Mother was appalled that women were becoming so ruthless--most especially a mother! In February, the even more infamous Bruno Richard Hauptmann was found guilty by a jury of his peers in Flemington, New Jersey for the kidnapping and murder of Charles Lindbergh's baby boy.

Roosevelt was still about putting in place yet another alphabet soup agency with his WPA, Works Program Administration. And, let us not forget the Social Security Act that FDR had signed into law on August 14, 1935.

Our Mother thought the new program would help the elderly who were without any savings or means of support. True, the churches had been one of the primary sources for the poverty-stricken and starving, but FDR found a clever way for the government to grow even more omnipotent.

Our Dad had taken an entirely different view of FDR's government-run program which he discussed a few years later. He saw the potential for a bureaucracy the likes of which no one would be able to control. He said that the Social Security program signed into law that August was neither the kind of approach nor program FDR had campaigned to implement.

Our Dad didn't trust those who ran government. While he believed the program would help those in stark poverty, he thought Roosevelt had found a way to take the Peoples' money by putting it into a huge account with the promise to pay the recipient upon his or her retirement. True, the recipient would receive not only his or her paid-in share, but also would be paid with dollars the recipient didn't pay into Social Security--if they lived long enough to collect it. There was no distinction between those who were at the lower end of the financial ladder, and those who were at the top, which Dad thought was a nondiscriminatory approach.

While Roosevelt *gave with one hand,* he *took with the other* by putting in play a federal payroll tax. He also signed the *Revenue Act of 1935*, also known as the *Wealth Tax Act,* which increased income tax rates for wealthy Americans and corporations. Unfortunately, nothing that FDR had done since taking office seemed to be working *for the People;* the Country continued in the grip of the *Great* Depression.

Not to be outdone, union organizers created the CIO, *Congress for Industrial Organization,* in November. Dad knew what the unions and Roosevelt were all about--but, I was only a thirteen-year-old child with little to no understanding of what our parents were talking about.

I do recall our Dad talking about the *Triangle Factory Fire,* which occurred in New York City on March 25, 1911 when Dad was twenty-one years old. As a boy, he and a school chum had loved being around fire stations but, on that March day our Dad saw the result of the inhuman working conditions the women at the Triangle Shirtwaist Company had suffered to earn a subsistence living. Prior to the fire, garment workers with Triangle walked out, joining 20,000 other workers, in their strike for better working conditions. Triangle had refused to sign the collective bargaining agreement.

Gaslights, no fire extinguishers, and flammable textiles were made to order for the disaster of untold proportions at the ten-story building housing the Triangle Shirtwaist Company on the top three floors of the Asch Building.

Our Dad described how he had stood on the corner of Washington Place and Greene Street in Manhattan and watched the trapped girls screaming from the ninth floor windows, then breaking out the windows and jumping to their deaths, their clothes in flames. The archaic fire trucks in 1911 were not outfitted with long enough ladders or hoses and so, the loss of life was inevitable.

Ira Gershwin, Irving Berlin, Jerome Kern, and Cole Porter were churning out songs for Broadway and Hollywood musicals that transported the people to another time and place--if only for a few hours. *Escape* seemed the only temporary elixir for the People.

Hollywood's leading man, Clark Gable, starred in *Mutiny On The Bounty.* Charlie Chan's weekly features held everyone's attention, while Ginger Rogers and Fred Astaire continued to dance into the Peoples' hearts and, of course, Shirley Temple remained everyone's darling with that year's films: *The Little Colonel, Our Little Girl,* and *Curly Top.* And Agnes sang *Animal Crackers in My Soup* for two weeks running!

There is one movie I shall always remember if, for no other reason but that Agnes and I were so touched by it. Mom and Dad had dropped us off at the Plaza Theater in Englewood while they went shopping. We sat watching *The Night Is Young,* staring Ramon Novarro, Evelyn Laye, and Rosalind Russell.

Ramon Novarro portrayed a Prussian soldier at the turn-of-the-century who had fallen in love with a ballet dancer. The beautiful Evelyn Laye had won the soldier's heart, leaving the other young lady to stand with the soldier's picture in her hand at the end of the movie singing, *When I Grow Too Old To Dream.* When our Dad came to collect us in the lobby, he frowned a look at us and said, "What's happened? What's the matter with you two?"

Through gushing tears, Agnes and I tried to explain why we were so sad and, of course, it was impossible. Dad smiled. "It was only a picture, girls. Sometimes a movie will be very happy or very sad because that's what Hollywood does. It's all make-believe," he said. "Stop crying and behave yourselves, this is foolish. Let's go have some ice cream, then go home."

It was the song that had touched us and made us think of little Alexander. The movies of our time were a far cry from the kind our youngsters are seeing today. First Amendment *Free Speech* rights did not protect sex and violence back then. Today, the courts have taken a different view, protecting the purveyors of immorality, indecency, and lewd and lascivious behavior. What has happened to society to have become so numb to the evil foisted on our young people?

Some time during 1935, WOR-Radio introduced *Uncle Don* (Carney) who read the comic strips to his audience of children, sang songs, told jokes, and announced listeners' birthdays. His opening song began: "Hello, little friends, hello. Hello nephews, nieces, too. Mothers and daddies, how are you? This is your Uncle Don all set to go with our meeting on the radio...This is your Uncle Don, your Uncle Don..."

February had been bitterly cold with lots of snow, and Agnes and I were home from school listening to John B. Gambling and Martin Block, whose broadcast was interrupted with a voice that began: "This is radio station WNEW coming to you from the little courthouse in Flemington, New Jersey, where the jury in the trial of Bruno Richard

Hauptmann has just found Hauptmann guilty of the kidnapping and murder of Charles Lindbergh's son..."

James Kilgallen and his daughter, Dorothy, both very popular reporters during the Thirties and Forties, had also covered the trial. (I recall that Dorothy Kilgallen was the reporter who, mysteriously, had been found dead following her 1965 interview with Jack Ruby, the man who killed Lee Harvey Oswald.)

Life returned to normal and Agnes and I continued to go to the Plaza Theater with our parents on Friday or Saturday evenings. Occasionally, we would go to a Sunday afternoon matinee by ourselves, having first reviewed the entertainment section of the paper to see which movie star's portrait was featured. We also read the *Katzenjammer Kids* comic strip, which was still funny to us as our Dad read about Mama, her twins, Hans and Fritz, and The Captain. *Dick Tracy,* held our attention for yet another week's episode to see how he would get out of the previous week's trouble.

The Crime of the Century was a cartoon version of the Lindbergh Trial which had been created to help people understand the complexity of the long and detailed trial which had become very difficult to follow. *Little Orphan Annie's* hardships seemed to override all the bad that existed in real life by showing us all how much worse life could have been--but, for the Grace of God!

Our Mother loved the Irish actor Pat O'Brien and that year we saw two of his motion pictures: *The Irish In Us* and *Oil for the Lamps of China.* We three would walk down to the Englewood Theater for the Wednesday afternoon matinee. A fifteen-cent adult ticket entitled the holder to a *free* giveaway. In the Spring, it was glazed pottery with a tea leaf pattern on the dinner plates, cups, and saucers. Later in the year, the *Shaunee* corn pattern was the promotional giveaway.

I made my Confirmation at St. Cecelia's and Aunt Rose, Mom's sister from New Rochelle, New York, came for the big event. (The Roman Catholic Church teaches that it is the sacrament of maturity and coming of age which complements and completes baptism. The effect of the sacrament of confirmation is to give strength in faith and for the confession of faith, and to impress an indelible character.) I can't help but believe that any child of an Irish Catholic mother indubitably possesses an *indelible character*--whether they want it or not.

Agnes and I became fans of the new NBC radio show, *Your Hit Parade* that began in April. The program featured all of the current top hits of the day and worked its "magic" that, somehow, encouraged us to go down to the record shop to buy the new release--at the very least, to listen to the new hits.

That was the year that the shy thirteen-year-old, Peter D'Alema (pronounced *dell-la-may*) set his sights on Agnes...

Just beyond Stelling's Ice Cream Parlor, a few doors down from the monument on West Palisade Avenue, was a small grocery store, called *D'Amadio's,* where our Mother occasionally shopped for fresh fruits and vegetables.

The skinny young boy who worked there always wore a bright white apron and was usually seen sweeping the sidewalk in front of the store. Mom, Agnes, and I had gone to matinee at the Plaza Theater and were walking up Palisade Avenue. As we approached the little grocery, the boy stopped sweeping and stood staring and grinning at Agnes (she told me later, in a quite agitated voice). His name was Peter D'Alema.

One afternoon in early Fall, Peter came riding his bike down Manhattan Avenue to our home. A basket attached to the handlebars of his bike was filled with fruits and vegetables that our Mother bought earlier in the day.

I remember that we made a lot of jelly and canned tomatoes that year. Peaches were selling for only ten cents a pound, producing as many as two dozen jars of jelly. We cooked the peaches, making an extra sweet thick syrup, which we saved to enjoy in the winter. Canning was the task that we ladies of the house worked in unison to accomplish. We helped wash and cut the fruits and vegetables, and made sure that the huge pot were always filled and the water boiling so the glass jars could be sterilized while Mom cooked the fruits. The jelly was much easier and I remember how careful she was in melting the paraffin wax that she poured over the newly-cooked jelly to make an airtight seal in the jars. Ketchup was another favorite we made.

Canning was usually done in late July through early September. Apples arrived in October which we either sliced and sprinkled with cinnamon to can for future pies, or we would make apple sauce. It was hard work, but so deliciously satisfying.

One of our Dad's coworkers and his wife often visited and, on a few occasions, Dad's friend brought along his guitar. Agnes was so infatuated with his guitar, that the couple offered to give Agnes formal guitar lessons. And so, they came and picked up Mom and Agnes and drove them to the instructor who introduced Agnes to the Hawaiian guitar. Her lessons lasted for nearly six months and she was progressing quite well, even to playing some songs in their entirety. Unfortunately, Dad's friend happened to mention that he had been divorced. And, the rest is history...

On August 15, 1935, the news broke that Will Rogers and his co-pilot, Wiley Post, were missing. Our parents had been very fond of Will Rogers' humor as Mom told Mr. Wurm that Thursday afternoon he came to see Dad about a *project*. She put on a pot of coffee while the radio announcer explained that the plane had been found in Alaska; both men had been killed.

After school one afternoon, Agnes and I were inspecting our Mother's new sewing machine. Well, in our curiosity of probing and lifting levers, the shaft holding the needle suddenly slammed down, straight into my finger and broke off. We frantically ran to a neighbor lady, who managed to calm us. She went for a basin of hot water and a bandage. She returned, held my arm around her so I couldn't see my hand and, somehow, pulled the needle out of my finger. When Mom came home, she went to the neighbor and thanked her for her help in dealing with our emergency. Everyone in the neighborhood respected her, as the grandmother she was, feeling confident that she could handle anything.

I was fine and, as a result, I decided that sewing machines were not for me. Agnes, however, was not discouraged and sat with Mom whenever sewing was the order of the day. My sister was considerably more persistent than me and her determination had her sewing little things within a few weeks. Agnes had a creative nature and enjoyed making doll clothes with detail that amazed us all.

1936

Unemployment was reported at 16.9%; the poverty level was established at $1,330; the *Great* Depression continued, and the Country (as the government told us) was in a *recession* by late summer!

Agnes was twelve and I turned fourteen in early October.

New York radio listeners were introduced to the *Green Hornet,* and Richard Bruno Hauptmann was executed for kidnapping and killing the Lindbergh baby. Bing Crosby sang *Pennies From Heaven,* Fred Astaire tap-danced to *The Way You Look Tonight,* and I hummed *Moon Over Miami*, wondering if the brilliant disk in the sky was shining as brightly over Miami as it was over Manhattan Avenue in West Englewood, New Jersey on those star-filled nights.

Roosevelt appointed an Irishman, named Joseph Kennedy, Sr., as U.S. Ambassador to Great Britain. England's King George V died in January and his son, Edward VIII, succeeded him. Instead of ascending to the throne, Edward announced his intention to marry the American divorcee, Wallis Simpson.

A month later, in December, he abdicated and became a "mock" commoner. Divorce was a rarity--not the norm as it has become today with nearly fifty percent of all marriages resulting in divorce. When we were growing up, marriage was *until death do us part.*

Hollywood introduced *Porky Pig* and *Mr. Deeds Goes To Town* with Jimmy Stewart. And *Life* Magazine appeared on the newsstands, providing wonderful pictures and stories on just about everybody and everything.

Dad came home from work one night excited and eager to tell us about seeing a "television" broadcast. None of us understood what he was talking about. It seems one of the stores on Van Brunt Street near the Plaza Theater had participated in running a test transmission for a broadcast company in New York which could be seen on a six-inch screen inside a little box. Television had already come into being; just not for the general populace. "Well, it won't be long before everyone will have one in their home," Dad had said. To which Mom replied: "Ye can start savin' yer money now, that way ye'll have enough in about twenty years!"

About this time, we began making more shopping trips into Hackensack, six miles away in the next town over, with many more stores than in little Englewood. We usually went for a day of shopping, which meant that we had the "treat" of eating lunch out. And because we were so accustomed to being *conservative*, lunch was usually in Woolworth's Five & Dime store where we had their "famous" hot dogs and foaming root beer in a frosty glass mug. I recall one Saturday after lunch, Agnes and I had our pictures taken in one of those photo machines. She wore a red-white-and-blue striped dress with a white brimmed Sailor hat. After the strip of photos popped out of the slot, Agnes said, "I don't feel so good." To which I teased: "Why? Don't you like your picture?"

When I think of those red-skinned hot dogs, I see the rows of interior columns that ran the length of the huge store and which were painted the same color as those hot dog skins. It's an odd memory, but a memory still of a day nearly seventy years ago.

We saw Eddie Cantor's *Suzy* which was a hit with Agnes. She and I also saw the movie, *Rose Marie. W*e spent hours trying to sing *Indian Love Call* as Nelson Eddy, the Canadian Mountie, had sung with his lovely co-star, Jeannette McDonald. Mom nearly had a fit, but our attempts at warbling those high notes only made her laugh! A good, hot cup of tea was duly earned as we sat around the kitchen table peeling potatoes for dinner.

When the Edna Ferber classic, *Show Boat* was released in 1936 as a musical, Agnes and I couldn't wait for it to open at the local theater in Englewood. We sat mesmerized as Irene Dunn, Allan Jones, Hattie McDaniel, and Paul Robeson carried our imaginations even deeper into South.

Is It True What They Say About Dixie? was another popular tune that year which continued our infatuation with the South. As I think back, I believe that our interest in the South began when Dad hired a black man, named Jackson, to do concrete work in the basement. His wife, Stella, was the sweetest lady we had ever met and who visited us often. She always offered to do some chores around the house, but our Mother refused to turn Stella's visit into any sort of indebtedness.

When Stella (we always called her Mrs. Jackson) first began visiting us, we used to giggle at her strange dialect. And, despite our mother's suggestion that Stella call her Margaret, the humble and steadfast woman always addressed her as *'Misses Walltah*.

Each time Stella stopped by, Agnes and I would sit with them at the kitchen table, all of us sipping our tea, while Stella shared her stories of how life was in the old South. As best as I can recall, she was born around 1875; the daughter of a former slave from South Carolina, where she had lived until she met and married Jackson. He was about five years younger than she, and both had moved to New Jersey sometime during the 1920s. He built a house on Shepherd Avenue, south of us. Whenever Stella's family sent her letters, I would read them to her, and then, write out her replies. She had the sweetest smile and always told our Mother: "Yo chil'in always knows wha' ah sez, Misses Walltah."

Years later, we realized how much Stella and our Mother had influenced our thinking. We saw two women from two distinctly different worlds enduring the hardships of the Depression years, equal as human beings, and trying only to survive.

Another five Shirley Temple movies were released that year...*The Littlest Rebel, Captain January, Poor Little Rich Girl, Dimples, and Stowaway*--all of which delighted us and filled yet five more afternoons with joy and happy thoughts. *The Littlest Rebel* seemed to captivated us the most because it was about the South. We always talked about one day traveling to the South but, in the meantime, we had to be satisfied with traveling to the local library to check out books about *Dixie, the land of cotton.*

Not a single girl from those years will ever forget the Shirley Temple doll and how absolutely crazy they were to have one. Unfortunately, there weren't any Shirley Temple dolls in any of the local stores in Englewood. The Hecht's Department Store in Manhattan carried them and I remember the day Agnes *finally* got her Shirley Temple doll...

Dad came home after working all day, got dressed up, (Agnes was waiting--already dressed in her peach-colored rayon crepe dress, white sox and shoes, and hat). They went into the city and bought her very own Shirley Temple doll. The doll, in its little red polka-dotted dress, came home in its cardboard box, along with the Shirley Temple pin Agnes proudly wore each and every day until she decided to save it, so nothing would happen to it.

Her affection for Shirley Temple was no different than any other little girl back then. I thought Agnes had carried her fascination to the limit. She started saving all the newspaper and movie magazine pictures of Shirley Temple that she could find to paste into her scrapbook. It has survived all these years, along with the little Shirley Temple pin, and are safely tucked away in Agnes' keepsake trunk.

While Agnes was always exceptionally young looking for her age, she was also exceedingly attractive, and very shy--unless she wanted her way. Dad used to say that Agnes was delicate, but no matter how *delicate* she was, he always chided her about how no one would ever guess that she had such an incredibly *short fuse*. But, that was part of her charm, as well--unless one was on the receiving end of that *charm*. You see, Agnes was just like Mom, and I was just like Dad.

When I look around today and see some twelve- and thirteen-year-old girls, the idea of even using the word *delicate* to describe them seems almost foreign to our language. Our children's lost innocence is one of the saddest realities of our current times. The sex and violence imposed on them is criminal. But, I remain hopeful and pray God that the People will stop abdicating their *rights* and start demanding accountability from their elected officials who remain *servants of the People*--NOT their lords and masters.

Girls and boys took to Agnes very easily in spite of her shyness, which was what everybody noticed first. Our childhood girlfriends were mostly Agnes' classmates because I was more the *loner* type and not very outgoing. I suppose I felt grown-up and wasn't particularly interested in other children. As for boys well, I viewed them as an *interruption*. I have to admit that I had been very protective of my sister, not just because our Mother had insisted that I take the initiative as the older sister, but because we had lost a baby brother and none of us wanted anything to happen to Agnes.

It was around late summer when my fears about Typhoid Fever began. I followed the news about Officer Jackson, an Englewood policeman, who had contracted the disease. The entire city turned out for his funeral, including us. A few weeks later, Health officials isolated the source of contamination to a brook on Booth Avenue in Englewood.

Officer Jackson was not the only case of Typhoid Fever that year, though the only fatality. A family came down with the dreaded disease, but all, miraculously, had overcome it. People were warned of the dangers of the highly communicable and deadly affliction. I recall noticing, even more than before, the Board of Health contagion signs posted on the front doors of homes when family members had been diagnosed with Measles, Whooping Cough, Scarlet Fever, and Dyptheria. My own fears increased significantly.

Mom sat me down at the kitchen table with a cup of tea one afternoon. Her nursing experience had instilled a kind of resistance to emotionality whenever she discussed illness and death, and she told me the story of Mary Mallon, the Irish immigrant known as *Typhoid Mary,* who had come to the United States in the late 1800s.

Mary Mallon lived in New York City at the turn of the century and was found to have been responsible for infecting dozens of people with Typhoid. She worked as a domestic and prepared the family food. *Typhoid Mary* managed to overcome her own bout with the disease, without knowing--or accepting--that she was a carrier.

The New York City health officials quarantined her in a hospital on North Brother Island and, again a year later, in 1915, where she spent the rest of her life until her death in 1938.

In late 1936, fear gripped the country as Wall Street's stocks began to decline again. The propagandists of the day started sending signals of a *recession* for 1937. In truth, we never got out of the Depression so, our parents questioned *how* the Country could be going into a *recession*! I guess no one was listening to that year's popular hit, *It's A Sin to Tell A Lie.*

The economy did heat-up to some degree, the result of European demands, but not so much so that the Country could notice. It was much later when the People actually realized it had been the result of a Europe gearing up for war.

There was no disputing the fact that the majority of the American People were dissatisfied with FDR--yet, he won re-election in a landslide victory that November in 1936, which gave him a resounding victory over Alfred (Alf) Landon. Roosevelt was on his way to a second term. I was only fourteen and knew I didn't like the man. There was something about him I just couldn't take; perhaps, it was the tone of his voice and pompous air that irritated me as I listened to his "fireside chats." Our parents thought it only fair that Roosevelt should have his chance to fulfill all of the promises he had made to the People.

One of the jokes of the day that our Dad loved to share was about Roosevelt's WPA: "Did you hear about the accident? The WPA guy got hurt leaning on his shovel... Yeah, it fell over!"

Hollywood kept churning out movies, one of which was *Follow the Fleet* with Dick Powell, who Agnes thought was the greatest. We seemed to be making more trips over the Seven Sisters to the Palisades to watch for ships sailing the Hudson River. She sent away for Dick Powell's autographed photo that year.

"I told you he would send me his photograph," she said the day his glossy photo arrived in the mail. "He even addressed it to me!" My reply: "Why don't you write for Roosevelt's picture if you're so sure of yourself!"

"Well, Margaret, Roosevelt would have to answer the request because so many people dislike him and because he's not particularly good-looking. Dick Powell doesn't have those problems!"

1937

Unemployment was reported at 14.3%. A first-class stamp still cost only three cents, and I'll always fondly remember how the postman delivered people's mail--*twice* a day, a morning and an afternoon delivery! In fact, I remember that the postman often returned our calls to let us know that a letter we had been waiting for had arrived and he would be *delivering it that afternoon!*

We've come a long way since those days--stamps now cost us thirty-seven cents each; mail is delivered once a day (if the conveyor systems don't trash the envelopes). and we're never bothered with a phone call to ask if they can expedite the delivery of a much anticipated letter!

Daffy Duck made his debut in the Spring. I remember, because Agnes and I walked all the way home trying to imitate the cartoon character's funny voice, which continued all the way through washing the dishes after dinner. Our Mother regretted that Hollywood had made such a movie, and we laughed harder still at her attempts to hide her own laughter!

We saw Dick Powell's *Singing Marine* and Walt Disney's *Snow White and the Seven Dwarfs* --yes, Agnes sang *Whistle While You Work* all the way home that day, too.

"You really don't have to whistle, Agnes. It's not ladylike."

"Everyone knows it's a song from *Snow White.*"

"Maybe so, but boys whistle--young ladies do not."

"Well, I know that," Agnes said. "I'm just practicing to whistle while I work at home!"

"I thought you'd be singing *Someday My Prince Will Come,"* I said as we passed the Monument.

"Margaret, princes don't come to Englewood. You should know that at your age."

Seventh Heaven with Jimmy Stewart introduced the song, *My Diane.* Agnes loved the song so much that she headed straight for the record shop where we searched until we found a copy. I can see her standing at the counter, waiting to pay the clerk, and saying that she wished her name was Diane.

Look Magazine had a new competitor in *Life* Magazine. There was talk about Howard Hughes' flight from Los Angeles to New York City (in seven hours and twenty-eight minutes), which utterly intrigued Agnes as she recalled the many times she sat in the neighbor's bi-plane. And Glenn Miller began his memorable career.

I also recall how elated our Mother was as she read her Irish newspaper with the news: "Well, leave it to the Irish to appreciate the sanctity of marriage!" she had said, sipping her tea, then reading aloud the paper's account of how the Irish had banned divorce under their new Constitution.

Our family physician, Dr. Walter L. Jordan, had detected a questionable heart beat in Dad in early February and wrote his superiors at the Public Service that he should be granted a leave of absence. The Public Service allowed a six-month medical leave with disability payments that amounted to *half* of his thirty-one-dollar weekly salary. Mom immediately placed an advertisement in the Bergen Evening Record for a position as a housekeeper with nursing experience so that she could compensate for Dad's lost wages.

I took charge of the calls that came in from the advertisement and discussed the family's needs. There were a good many small businesses, operated by both husband and wife, so the response was significant. I told them the hours my Mother was available and the rate of pay she charged. I then made a schedule, listing each family, their address, and the various tasks she would be doing.

Around the end of March, Mom developed a serious throat infection. It came on quite suddenly on a Friday afternoon. When there was no improvement by Saturday morning, we called Doctor Jordan who came right over. He examined her and said he was going to have to lance her throat because of the infection. He told Dad to "take the little one and busy yourselves out in the yard, or someplace. I'm keeping Margaret here to assist me."

Oh, my heavens, what do I know about lancing a throat?

Doctor Jordan explained what he was going to do, then proceeded to open his black medical bag, as he asked me to get a basin of water. When I returned, he sterilized his hands and the scalpel, sprayed Mom's throat with something, then began the relatively quick procedure of lancing her throat.

The operation went quickly enough; he then reassured Mom she would be alright, left a prescription for the sulfur drug which came as white powder, premeasured in little paper folds in a box. The directions were the contents of one fold had to be dissolved in water and given to her during the first twenty-four hours. He told me to check her temperature, keep the room comfortably warm, do not give her any solid foods, and keep checking on her every few hours.

"I want you to do exactly as I've explained, Margaret. And, the medicine must be given every four hours, along with the pain medication, as I've noted on the bottle."

He put such trust in me, instructing me to call immediately if anything didn't *look right*. Thank God, there were no complications and Mom recovered beautifully and returned to her work. She enjoyed meeting the families and tending to their children's needs.

I seemed to recall that Doctor Jordan's house call was only three dollars(!) and, he probably had to wait until our Dad's payday to collect it. Pride was the hallmark of those in professions who provided lifesaving care for those who were ill.

Around seven o'clock in the evening on May 6, 1937, the radio announcer broke into programming to carry the "live" reporting of the air ship disaster at Lakehurst, New Jersey. The *Hindenburg*, built by Germany's Zeppelin Company, had just flown across the Atlantic only to explode in flames as it prepared to dock at Lakehurst. There was talk and speculation for months after the disaster that it might have been sabotage, or even lightning. No definitive conclusion had been reached.

"God have mercy on those poor souls," Mom said, drying her hands in the dish towel as Agnes and I ran outside. We didn't have any sense of how far we were from Lakehurst as we looked up into the darkening sky, thinking we could see the glow from the crash. We read all the newspaper accounts about the *Hindenburg,* which had been the biggest air ship ever built, and nearly as long as the *Titanic.*

Agnes was voted the *Prettiest Girl* in school that Spring of 1937, and was chosen to design the front cover of the school yearbook, which our parents thought quite an honor and distinction for their thirteen-year-old daughter.

Hollywood's Jean Harlow died that June and our Mother's only comment, as I recall, was that the twenty-six year old actress was very beautiful, but she had lived a *very fast life*. She stared at me and said that I was looking very grown up. And, of course, well I should, I was nearly fifteen.

That afternoon, we walked down to Englewood to see "*Maytime*" with Nelson Eddy and Jeannette McDonald; in fact, we saw the movie twice--Mom paid the adult price for my ticket, hence, four pieces of the theater's giveaway china!

The three of us left the Plaza Theater for our walk up Palisade Avenue and, there he was, young Peter D'Alema, grinning and staring at Agnes as we approached *D'Amadio's* grocery store. I remember the sharp stare Agnes leveled on him.

"What is *he* looking at," Agnes asked, her gaze fixed down on the sidewalk.

"Well, he's not looking at Mom or me!"

Our Mother nodded to him with a smile and said: "He's only givin' ye a harmless smile, Agnes," she said.

Before school opened that Fall, our Mother decided we should have our hair done and the fashion of the day was to get a permanent, then the style could be combed as we chose. She had taken note of the beauty school in Hackensack and the young, aspiring beauticians who cut and permed hair as part of their learning experience and, of course, for a reduced fee. It was a new experience for us and we even thought we might like to be hair dressers someday.

Our Sunday afternoons were usually quiet ones and, with Mom out working, we waited dinner until she came home in the early evening. Agnes was roller skating with her friend, Ruthie, on Washington Place one Sunday afternoon in October, when her skate caught on a jagged piece of concrete. She fell, gashed her lip on the cement curb, and came home crying, her mouth covered with blood that gushed down her chin and onto her clothes. I panicked, but Dad took charge. "Let's clean it up," he had said, then called Doctor Jordan, who came right over that Sunday afternoon.

(Once upon a time, doctors made house visits--but that was before insurance companies mandated *managed care,* and before physicians affiliated with hospitals and became *corporations*.)

Doctor Jordan stitched up Agnes' lower lip that had grown horribly swollen, and then, he sent Dad down to the drugstore to have her prescription filled. She had to keep a bandage on her lip for a couple of weeks and, oh, how she continually asked how badly it *really* looked. She hardly ate or drank anything.

Then came the day when we walked down to Englewood for her appointment with Doctor Jordan. His office was in his home on Engle Street. He removed the stitches and showed Agnes how perfectly she had healed. She was quite self-conscious about the faint scar on her lower lip, and her slightly chipped front tooth. (Not to be outdone, I chipped a tooth three years later while working at Burnt's Bakery!) Luckily, the resulting scar never did take away from her appearance.

As traumatic as the roller skating accident had been, it didn't deter Agnes--especially since she had gotten a pair of ice skates for Christmas, along with a very pretty red snow suit. I couldn't roller skate or ice skate, couldn't even stand up on the things--and never wanted to! But, I stood in the cold and watched Agnes skate and remember how I called out to her, "Don't ya think we ought to leave now?"

I seemed to recall that my sister's interest in ice skating might have begun right after we saw the young Norwegian ice skater, Sonja Henie, who starred in the movie, *One in a Million*, about an Olympic ice skater (of course). Later, we saw the handsome Tyrone Power opposite Sonja Henie in the movie, *Thin Ice.*

On those afternoons after school when Agnes finished ice skating, we always stopped into the little store at the corner of Washington Place and Teaneck Road that sold candy and ice cream. Local school boys usually hung around the corner talking, as young boys do. It was around this time that I was nicknamed, "the chaperone," mainly because I *discouraged* their attempts to talk with Agnes. After all, she wasn't quite fourteen--and, our Mother always expected a report of our day's activities when she came home.

Dad resumed his full-time work schedule and Mom decided that because Agnes and I were "maturing quite nicely" and were capable of caring for ourselves and the house, she was going to continue to work. She loved children and felt that she could do what she had done best--care for children. She was employed by the Delabo family in West Englewood to care for their two sons, one of whom became a doctor who, in later years, treated our parents.

Following the Eddie Cantor Show one Sunday evening, was a new program, called the *Mr. Anthony Show*. It was a very unusual format because people wrote letters to *Mr. Anthony*, asking his advice. The announcer began reading a listener's letter: "Dear Mr. Anthony, I met a man a year ago..." and Mr. Anthony gave his advice. The announcer proceeded with another letter: Dear Mr. Anthony, there's this young woman I recently dated..."

Agnes and I laughed at the ridiculous (and comical) problems people had asked Mr. Anthony to solve. As I reflect back on that radio show, I suppose it wasn't so different from the *Dear Abbey* columns, or the *Doctor Laura* show of today. Of course, the *kind* of situations that burden today's generation would have been much too shocking (and too private) for the public's consumption back then.

1938

Thanks for the Memory was a big hit that year as unemployment went back up to 19.1% with Federal spending reported at $6.84-Billion. *Superman* made his debut, Shirley Temple gave us *Rebecca of Sunnybrook Farm,* while Bing Crosby sang *I've Got a Pocketful of Dreams* which pretty much summed it up for the People.

Most everyone talked about the German troops that marched into Austria early that year. By Springtime, the Nazis occupied Austria, and our parents were convinced war was on the horizon. Though they tried not to alarm us, we couldn't help hearing their conversations.

Roosevelt signed the Fair Labor Standards Act which raised the minimum wage from twenty-five cents an hour to forty cents an hour and which also limited the work week to forty-four hours. Granted, it was *better than nothing* for those who *had nothing,* and it did stop employers from paying employees *next to nothing.*

The Revenue Act reduced taxes on large corporations and *raised* taxes on small businesses. Here we are sixty-seven years later, and corporations now have the government's blessing to eliminate the "minimum wage" altogether by having their products manufactured in countries where there is no minimum wage--only "slave labor."

Agnes turned fourteen and started Confirmation classes at St. Cecelia's. So did her quiet admirer, Peter D'Alema, who sat at the back of the class, staring and grinning as he had been doing the last four years.

I remember Agnes coming home after each class complaining to the heavens how "All he ever does is stare at me!" (I might have used the expression, "Get over it!" if it had been part of our lexicon.*)* But the truth is the truth, nearly everyone stared at Agnes. We were accustomed to seeing the way people seemed to be caught up in the blue of her thick-lashed eyes and dark brunette hair which were quite dramatic against her white skin. (By now, you've determined that I was very proud--and very protective--of my sister.)

We walked to Miller's Pond on the Dwight Morrow High School property in Englewood so that Agnes could ice skate--while I froze--until winter released its hold and the pond *finally* melted. She had me at a disadvantage; I couldn't get to her on the slippery ice and, hence, couldn't discourage the boys who skated around her and then stopped to hold conversation with her. Through all of my overprotectiveness, Agnes never complained and, well she could have; we both knew my instructions came from on high--our Victorian-thinking Mother, and understood the *consequences* if we disobeyed her.

Tuesdays were Dad's payday; which meant going to Big Bear to shop for the week's food. It was the first "supermarket" to come to our town and was located on Cedar Lane in Teaneck, We went to Hackensack more often, stopping into Sears & Roebuck on Anderson Street, which was the continuation of Main Street as you crossed the Hackensack River. The Sears building, was a grand-looking department store, constructed in the Art Deco style of the late 1920s and early 1930s. It had something for everyone, including a wonderful coffee shop. It was fun just "to look." Naturally, we had accustomed ourselves to *looking*, rather than buying just to buy. There had to be a need and money enough to pay for it.

Deanna Durbin's new movie, *That Certain Age,* featured a dress that came to be known as the "bicycle dress" made in a deep blue fabric, its skirt designed with white panels filled with polka dots. As expected, young girls clamored to have one. Agnes found out that Deanna Durbin's *bicycle dress* was available at Macy's in New York, and Mom sent off a money order. It would be her Confirmation gift.

Neither of us had a bicycle, but one of Agnes' friends who lived up the hill on Washington Place, had one. Ruthie shared her bicycle with Agnes, riding throughout our secluded little neighborhood, Spring, Summer, and Fall while I raked and dug in the garden with Mom--and loved it! I recall picking string beans, still warm from the summer sun, bunches of carrots, and ears of corn from the stalks in the few little rows that were planted.

Memorial Day was always a *big* day in town, beginning early in the morning, when people lined both sides of the Palisade Avenue parade route, from the Monument all the way downtown. Despite the hard times, people of all nationalities took pride in showing their patriotism and love for America and the men who gave their lives preserving this Country. All the stores closed on Memorial Day, except restaurants and soda fountains. And everyone dressed up in their finest; men and boys wore suits and ties; and women and girls wore dresses, silk stockings (girls wore sox), hats, and gloves.

Agnes and I often talked about that Memorial Day in 1938 which we always said was the most memorable of all we had experienced... She and I went ahead of our parents, arriving at the Monument as the Spanish-American War Veterans slowly marched down the center line on Palisade Avenue.

We heard talk that 1938 marked the 75th Anniversary of the Battle of Gettysburg and that the few surviving veterans of that battle were going to meet to commemorate that historic event. The celebration had a special meaning for us. It may have been all the stories that Stella Jackson shared with us or, perhaps, the five-thirty Sunday evening WABC-Radio broadcast of *Roses and Drums,* with *Captain Randy* which seemed to encapsulate us in those long ago yesteryears. Even now, I see our Dad sitting in his rocker, listening to the radio drama.

On a Sunday afternoon in June, Agnes (and Peter) made their Confirmation. Mom, Dad, and I sat in the front pew of the church watching the procession of newly confirmed young Roman Catholics. Mom recognized Peter as he walked to the altar, and smiled. Agnes rolled her eyes disapprovingly.

Peter was 16-years old, six months older than I. Agnes was fourteen. He was definitely *smitten* with her, no one would dispute that. He would nod at her whenever he saw her, not just whenever we passed by the grocery store where he worked, but in the theater as well. Somehow, he would be sitting a few rows in front, or behind us--gazing and grinning.

Later that summer, Mom allowed me to take a part-time job with an elderly German couple who lived on Westerville Place in West Englewood. The husband had retired several years before and helped his wife with some of the house cleaning because she used a cane and didn't get around very well. They hired me to help with light house chores. The lady would sit at her kitchen table preparing vegetables for the main meal which they ate late in the day.

One afternoon, I accidentally knocked a box of *Rinso* Soap Powder off of the shelf above the kitchen sink; spilling onto her freshly washed and cut string beans. I thought, *Oh well, this is the end of this job*!

I apologized and she said: "Don't you worry about it; Margaret, they have to be well washed and the powder will not hurt them." And then added, "It could happen to anyone; the box was misplaced," she said, standing at the sink, one hand on the cane, the other rinsing the beans all over again.

At the end of each day, the lady always said, "Before you walk home, Margaret, have your juice and cookies." They paid me forty-five cents for an hour's work, though the part-time wage was twenty-five cents an hour. Sometimes, I would work a full two hours and they would give me a little more, not double, but a little more. At sixteen, I felt content that I was not only accomplishing something, but also had an organized and productive day. I can see myself walking home one pleasant Autumn afternoon, a distance of only a mile-and-a-quarter from where we lived, and how good I felt having a job. I was *finally* grown up, or so I thought.

Tragedy visited us again, on September 30, 1938...

I was walking home from school that afternoon, by way of Washington Place, when throngs of people came walking up the hill in my direction. Ann, one of our school friends, was waiting for me at the top of the hill. She tried to break the news as delicately as she could, but I rushed for home, only to find a row of fire trucks blocking Manhattan Avenue. Mom had gone to meet Agnes at her school.

Snake-like tubes of hosing crisscrossed the yard as a dozen men in black rubber-coated canvas coats wearing hip-high black boots aimed their silvery nozzles on the last crackling flares that fought to maintain their hold. The Fire Marshall told us the flames had started on the second floor, in the clothes closet in the front bedroom that Agnes and I shared. He suspected a shorted-out electrical line to the closet light fixture.

The entire top floor, roof and walls, were gone. Only charred wood studding stood as failed sentinels under leaf-covered limbs denying the light of day. Flares of fire relinquished their fight under water-soaked, crumbling walls while puffs of smoke gave confirmation that the siege was over. Rivers of water flowed down onto the window panes on the main level, over furniture, walls, and floors blanketed with black soot from the flaming inferno above.

When all but one of the fire trucks pulled away, and the sightseers had seen the last of the disaster, only a few friends remained as we stood dazed and unable to rationalize what had happened.

Agnes and I looked down through our tears as we stood on the drenched walkway alongside the house. There strewn across the narrow path lay our sodden and scorched Holy Communion veils, and our burned and shattered beds and bureau that we had since childhood... all my books and magazines... and gone were all of Agnes' dolls. Tears streamed down Agnes' face as she fell to her knees and lifted the melted remains of her Shirley Temple doll. The pin, still in its tiny metal container, had survived the flames that stole Shirley and Agnes' other childhood companions.

The remnants of our clothes lay smoldering on the walkway, leaving only the clothes we were wearing. Ann tried to comfort us as she stood between us, her arms around our shoulders. I knelt to pick up one of the dresses; it disintegrated in my hands, the shreds falling to the walkway. Our furnishings, our clothes, all of our keepsakes; Mom's photo albums, Dad's collectibles and books, and especially Alexander's toys and mementos... were lost.

On a patch of grass beyond the narrow path lay Agnes' Shirley Temple scrapbook. We never understood *how* it was spared from the flames and water. But survive it did, along with so many memories; the only survivors of time locked in the solitary confines of my mind.

The home our parents worked so tirelessly to build, improve, and maintain stood in its humbled defiance. It had only been a few years since they completed the last of the renovation. Now they had to start over again; too proud to give up, never carrying a mortgage on the house--and not about to start--though they did take out a reconstruction loan.

We had experienced how unexpectedly our lives had changed following Alexander's death, but this tragedy was something else entirely. It was as if the past had never happened; what took its place was an uncertainty that invaded each one of us, challenging our will to survive the cataclysm.

Mom stiffened her back: "Nothing is forever and only faith will get us through the worst of this," she said, as the last fire truck drove down Manhattan Avenue. Stella took Mom's hand, patted it, and insisted that we go stay with her; "Jackson is down South with his people." We stayed with Stella just short of a week; she fed us and gathered up clothes for us from some of our neighbors.

Our parents were grateful for Stella's loving concern and hospitality, and before Jackson returned from his trip, our parents rented two rooms from a neighbor lady for the long duration of reconstruction ahead of us.

Our Mother and Father arranged for us to be home from school the following week which allowed us to spend afternoons in Englewood shopping the stores for the things our parents said we would need. Now was the time for us to grow up.

This was also the week Agnes decided she was going to buy some makeup. It started with a tube of *Tangee* lipstick and finished with my wearing a glass of buttermilk--all over a beautiful blue crepe dress. Our Mother did not approve of the lipstick. It was my responsibility to have known that she never would have condoned fourteen-year-old Agnes wearing *any* makeup. But Agnes was quite proud, and just owning that little tube of lipstick made all the difference in the world to her.

"I'm grown-up," she said, her words coming with an undeniable certainty.

"*You're* grown-up? I'm the one who wore the buttermilk!"

"I didn't make you wear it," she said.

"Well, I don't own any lipstick so, it *must* have been your fault!"

That little tube of lipstick signaled the start of Agnes getting more than just a "little fussy" about what she would and wouldn't wear, and how she should look. She started sewing her own dresses and, occasionally, mine as well. I couldn't figure out the dress patterns no matter how long I inspected the dots and lines on the flimsy paper pieces. The ease with which she followed the instructions, somehow, enabled her to draw her own pattern designs, copying *exactly* any dress she saw. The number of her girlfriends increased; they, too, hoped to share in Agnes' talents, at the very least, with a new dress she would make for them out of the fabric they provided.

The rebuilding of the old house began in mid-October and by mid-November we moved back home, though the house was not nearly finished. Only a new roof and walls on the second level were constructed. There was painting and wallpapering to be done on all the new walls in the rooms and halls, staining the new pine floors upstairs, as well as refinishing all the first-level pine floors that had been water soaked. Mr. Wurm and Jackson were always by Dad's side, helping with the work the contractors were not engaged to do.

Agnes and I helped as much as we could after school and on the weekends, we shopped almost everyday to replace linens and the things we knew how to buy for our parents who couldn't take any more time away from their jobs.

The sacrifices through the Depression years had taken their toll on our parents' generation. Those who grew up during those years of hardship and denial matured with an ingrained sense of responsibility and obligation, which has never been extinguished.

1939

Of the dozens of wonderful songs released that year, the Country enjoyed *Roll Out The Barrel* and *Beer Barrel Polka,* both of which seemed appropriate with all of the Federal "*pork barrel*" Spending that reportedly climbed to $9.14-Billion. Unemployment came down two points to 17.2% which gave new meaning to the song, *T'aint What You Do...it's the way that you do it!*

The World's Fair opened in January in New York City and Roman Catholics celebrated their new Pope, Pius XII. The *SS St. Louis*, carrying nine-hundred-sixty-three Jewish refugees from Europe, was turned away from Florida, as Cuba also had done, resulting in its return to Europe and a fate neither they, nor the world could have envisioned.

Hedda Hopper joined Jimmy Fiddler and Walter Winchell, who kept everybody apprised of still more Hollywood gossip--which provided a continuing diversion from the pressing issues of the day. David O. Selznick released Margaret Mitchell's *Gone With The Wind* in Atlanta, Georgia with its stars, Clark Gable, Vivian Leigh, Olivia de Havilland, Leslie Howard, and Hattie McDaniel on hand for the grande world premiere. When the movie finally opened in Manhattan, lines of theatergoers overflowed the sidewalks for weeks afterward.

Harry James formed his own band that year and Frank Sinatra took center stage as his vocalist; and the girls swooned. (Agnes did; I did not!)

The Wizard of Oz was also released that year which gave Agnes and two of our girl friends new song and dance material. They sang *If I Only Had a Brain* (I silently agreed while watching them imitate *Dorothy*, the *Tin Man,* the *Cowardly Lion*, and the *Strawman),* as we walked the Seven Sisters to the Palisades.

Music had made a big impression on us since 1935, and even more so with the ever-increasing popularity of the Big Bands. This was especially so for Agnes. Her personality seemed to be well-defined by the time she reached fourteen. Her interest in art began to blossom in a multitude of ways. The money she had saved from the "rag man" was used to buy art magazines of the classics. Her teachers were always asking her to take on a project that enabled her to utilize her art skills. One of her teachers recommended a retired art instructor to our parents who decided to invest in advanced art lessons for her.

Barbara, one of Agnes' school chums, also had an interest in art and music. She lived at the Teaneck Armory with her grandparents. Her grandfather was the custodian responsible for maintaining the nearly fourteen-acre complex. Construction started in 1936 and, if memory serves me, was completed in 1938 for nearly one-million dollars.

Barbara invited Agnes to visit when National Guardsmen practiced their marching formations and, sometimes, when their military band played military marching songs during their drills. The two girls also went ice skating together through the winter months. Barbara came for dinner quite often and, afterwards, we would walk her back to the Armory, up Liberty Road, the same road General Washington had traveled during the Revolutionary War.

Germany and Italy signed their *Pact of Steel* which, ultimately, allowed them to "steal" as much of Europe as they wanted. Hungary and Spain withdrew from the League of Nations, and the Soviet Union was expelled from the organization for attacking Finland later in the year.

Events were clearly in motion, as I reflect back on so many things. Germany's Hitler and the Soviet Union's Stalin signed their own *Pact* to divide up Eastern Europe, while our radios played: *Lili Marlene, Somewhere in France With You, There'll Always Be An England,* and *Til the Lights of London Shine Again.* The politicians must have been convinced the whole of the Country was *Somewhere Over the Rainbow!*

We were nearing the last of the renovation in the house. Our Dad rented a sanding machine to refinish that wonderful pine flooring that he purchased from the salvage company in Englewood. They had removed the flooring from a Victorian home in the prestigious Englewood Cliffs.

Agnes and I helped paint the walls and baseboards, as well as doing the wallpapering--with Ann's help. One day as she was leaving for her part-time job, she stopped at the door, turned around to us, and said: "Now, you two, leave everything where it is because I don't want the place ruined!" Ann was special and nearly as close as a sister to us.

Before the new appliances were brought in, Agnes and I helped Dad lay the linoleum in the kitchen. Our "new" kitchen had turned out beautifully with bright white cabinets, a double porcelain sink, and a six-light window above. Starched white curtains, trimmed with a border of green flowers, danced in the cool Autumn breezes.

We were home the day all the new appliances arrived; a brilliant white refrigerator, stove, and washing machine. Clothes dryers were available, but they were expensive and we didn't really mind hanging the clothes out on the clothes line.

Mom, Agnes, and I sat at the new kitchen table having our tea and slice of pound cake on the new kitchen dishes. The deep blue of the saucer against the snow white table top was picture-perfect for a magazine ad. Oh, how our Mother was fond of "reading the tea leaves," especially when our friends came and we all sat around the table. "There's a letter coming to ye... and, yes, I see a very special gift for ye on yer birthday..." or whatever holiday was approaching.

On another afternoon sitting with our Mother having tea, she said, "I was reading in the paper that if we could change our being, from human to an animal, it would tell a lot about our personality." I chose a racehorse, which Mom interpreted as a personality anxious to take control. Agnes chose a bird, which conveyed a personality content with her environment and that she was happy.

After nearly a year of working for the German couple who were very sweet and generous, I took a position with a lovely younger couple who had a seven-year-old daughter for whom Mom had cared. I was to babysit their little girl after school and do light chores around the house. I was there mainly to make sure that their little girl was accountable for what she was doing and to monitor where she went. It required longer hours, but it was steady work and there would be a little more money in my paycheck at the end of the week.

The father was in real estate and his wife commuted into Manhattan each day to her job. They didn't live too far from my high school so, it was convenient for me to be there for their little girl until one of her parents came home. They had given me a key to their house and I went directly there after school and did whatever tidying-up needed to be done. The mother would leave instructions for some food preparation, and I would set the dining room table for their supper.

One of the things I'll always remember about that job is that they had one of those newly-advertised three-piece pot sets. (Of all the things to stick in one's mind!) The style had garnered considerable attention because each of the individual pots had been designed as a pie wedge with a slanted and curved top so that all three pots could connect to form one pot. Efficiency began to take hold; instead of three burners heating three individual pots, one burner could do the work of three.

It did seem practical and, of course, I was all for practicality. (I suppose it wouldn't surprise you if I said that I really was a *fusspot* in my teens!) At seventeen, I began to see the purpose in life and the things that could help achieve those objectives.

Sometimes, I took the clothes from the line outside and folded them; dusted the furniture throughout the house, or pushed the carpet-sweeper over their area rugs. It was an old-fashioned house with lots of fine wood furniture. When the family moved to Elizabeth Street, closer to Teaneck High School, I thought my position had been made even more secure. But, alas, I was always looking to improve myself, and obtained other more challenging work---with more money, of course.

Our home was fully renovated by the time Spring arrived. Our parents allowed us to choose our new bedroom furniture. Agnes selected a long, low dresser with a mirror that ran the full width of it. She decided that the wide dresser was perfect to hold her toiletries. I, on the other hand, chose a chest of drawers--it was utilitarian; besides, I didn't see the point in having two dressers cluttering the room and consuming two walls.

On occasion, I would borrow Agnes' perfume or stockings, which made her furious. We had always shared our money to buy whatever either of us needed. "What's the harm in my borrowing," I asked. "Buying *one* of whatever we need, instead of *two* is being thrifty," I said. Agnes didn't see the logic in that--only that I was being *ridiculously frugal*!

"Then, you better mark on the calendar exactly which days you'll be wearing the stockings--and, make sure you mark the day you run them, so you have a new pair for me to wear the next day."

From Spring through late Fall, I remember an outdoor fruit and vegetable market at the crossing of West Street and Palisade Avenue. During the Spring, rows of wooden stands tilted forward with their smorgasbord of produce and flowers. In the Fall, their stands showcased the medley of decorative greenery for the Christmas season.

One stall, owned by Italians, always carried White Gardenias which we particularly liked. At least a half-dozen Saturdays in Springtime, we purchased our twenty-five cent White Gardenias, pinning them to the collars of our blue coats so we could enjoy their fragrance that danced in the sassy Spring air. It made an ordinary day more special than it otherwise might have been.

(I'm sure the thought has occurred to you that we two teenage girls were spending *two* hour's wages on two flowers during those days of hard times... Yet, here we are today with teenagers who not only have a good deal more money to spend, but who have access to illicit drugs and sex paraphernalia on which to spend it! It makes me so sad.)

Peter D'Alema had finally gotten up enough nerve to talk to

Agnes whenever he saw her, and she did behave a little more friendly toward him. He had asked her if he may be permitted to come visit her at our home. She nodded and said, "Yes. I think that would be alright." After all, her *chaperone*--would be there. Our parents didn't see any harm in his visiting; they had known the boy all the years he had worked at the little grocery store downtown.

Peter's visits to our home soon turned into invitations to meet him at the Plaza Theater where, as an usher, he was allowed "free admissions" for family and a few friends. It was hardly a date. As long as I was there *to chaperone*, our parents didn't see the harm in Agnes meeting Peter at the theater as his "guest."

I recall that rainy Friday, September 1, 1939... Agnes and I decided to stay home from school that day. I was sitting in the rocking chair, looking at a magazine, as the radio played; Agnes was studying. The rain seemed unending, and then the newscaster interrupted the music: *Hitler's German troops have invaded Poland--the people are now under Nazi occupation.* I thought, *how long will it be before our men and boys go off to war?*

Father Charles E. Coughlin's political support for Roosevelt had taken a complete reversal over the last few years. The radio priest took to calling the President, *"Franklin Double-Crossing Roosevelt,"* with vociferous attacks calling Roosevelt an *anti-God* and *Communist*.

The day before my birthday, our parents returned from Englewood with a birthday cake, when a call came from Mom's brother. Aunt Molly, his wife, had died. The news hit our Mother terribly. As she frantically packed for their trip to New Rochelle where they would be staying through the funeral service, Dad gave me some money and detailed the instructions for *our* trip to New Rochelle the next morning. Agnes and I would pack a few things, lock-up the house in the morning, making certain there were no lights burning, and catch the brown bus at Knickerbocker Road that would take us over the George Washington Bridge, and into the City. I wrote down Dad's instructions, underlining his directions that we get off at the Third Avenue Trolley where we would take the subway to connect with another bus for the ride to New Rochelle.

One Friday afternoon a week or two later, we walked to Knickerbocker Road, boarded that brown bus that crossed over the George Washington Bridge, and took the subway to Broadway--the heart of the theater district. We stood in line for what seemed hours to buy our tickets for the early evening show at the Paramount Theater and, on that late October day, Agnes and I sat in awe as the audience of young people applauded Glenn Miller's Big Band and the Ink Spots who sang *If I Didn't Care*.

After the show, Agnes wanted to buy a pair of shoes in the Ansonia Shoe Store on Broadway. I told her that their shoes were more expensive than Miles Shoe Store, but she was quick to tell me that their styles were considerably more beautiful and certainly worth the difference. I think I even bought a pair that early evening.

We also stopped into a Chockful 'O Nuts restaurant where we had a cup of coffee. If time permitted, we would stop by the Church of the Holy Cross on 42nd Street. Agnes and I always loved the look of the old brick and mortared wall that had been erected in 1852, its interior representative of the mid-Victorian era.

On one such visit I remember every electric light had been turned off and only flickering candles glowed throughout the venerable interior during Benediction service. I can still see the church, as if it were yesterday and recall how special the church was to our Mother. Reverend Francis P. Duffy, the new Rector in 1921, was a Chaplain with the *Fighting Irish* 69th Regiment of New York whom New Yorkers honored with a statue in Times Square.

Monsignor Joseph McCaffrey followed Father Duffy's tenure. He, too, had been a Chaplain with the 69th Regiment and had distinguished himself with a Silver Star and France's *Croix de Guerre.* Our Mother often told us how she had attended services at Holy Cross and known father McCaffrey prior to World War I, remembering him going off to war in his uniform as a Lieutenant Colonel. New York City, likewise, honored Father McCaffrey and dedicated a park to him on West 43rd Street.

Today, however, the Ten Commandments--even God Himself--are being taken from public view. What's to be gained by attacking God?

We would make many, many more trips to Broadway, returning to the Paramount and the other Broadway theaters to see Glenn Miller, Tommy and Jimmy Dorsey, Benny Goodman, along with the other Big Bands that had begun to make our heart's sing.

In the autumn of 1939, our school friends, Dorothy and Kay, joined us for "shopping" trips, making our little group four. We strolled through the stores in Englewood--again, always *looking,* as opposed to buying. We spent Saturdays roaming through the dime store trying on costume jewelry and the like. We might buy a pair of shoes at Miles for two dollars and a pair of silk stockings for fifty-nine cents. You see, every "well dressed" young lady wore stockings, gloves, *and* a hat. Stockings were made with dark seams up the entire length of the back of the legs. The challenge was in keeping the seams perfectly straight at all times.

One memory I have from those Saturday afternoon shopping excursions is seeing two Sisters of Charity, our teaching nuns at St. Cecelia's. They always walked in two, wearing crisp white habits, as they smiled and nodded to passersby. Seeing those Nuns always made our day; perhaps, it was the rightness of everything they had taught us in the forever necessity of being dignified and doing what was proper. Their delicate demeanor and pristine personage set them apart from my generation of women. I think of all the generations of habited women who endured the hardships of their calling, but whose lives provided incalculable inspiration. Sadly, the absence of habited Nuns today is also unreckonable.

Life was simple for young people in those days and socializing had its place. Although girls discussed which boy they'd like to date, it remained their parents' decision to sanction dating. Boys we had known throughout our childhood were growing into manhood and learning how to flirt. Yes, *all the boys flirted with Agnes* and, yours truly was always there to make certain they didn't get unruly or behave inappropriately. If we were downtown as dusk set in, it was quite common to see a group of young people standing under a light pole, talking and joking. I will admit, we had been duly warned by our parents: "Don't let me catch you girls standing under the light pole," our Dad said. "Or it'll be the divil ye'll be gettin," Mom confirmed.

Miller's Pond, near the Dwight Morrow High School, was a natural meeting place for young people during the winter skating months. Most teen-aged boys did not have access to cars, and curfew was generally at ten o'clock. Children were respectful and obeyed *the rules*. There was no government interference--or fear of reprisals--if parents chastised their child.

(The main difference between "then" and "now" is that, today, parents tend to pat their children on their backs, when they should be patting a whole lot lower and harder. Government intrusion has compromised the family and usurped parental authority. I'd also like to see some government gumption and restraints placed on the judiciary who should not be rewarding sex offenders with a "Get Out of Jail" card so they can continue abusing and murdering innocent children.)

On those windy, overcast winter days, we usually walked to Stelling's Ice Cream Parlor, not for ice cream, but for a hot chocolate. (In summer, we usually ordered a *phosphate*. A phosphate was a delicious combination of seltzer water, milk, crushed ice, and plenty of chocolate, or vanilla, or strawberry syrup.)

Late that year, as Agnes approached her sixteenth birthday, our parents allowed her a Sunday afternoon "date." One young man came to our home and he and Agnes would walk downtown to the Theater to see a show. I have to laugh about one Sunday afternoon date... Ann came over to see Agnes, who was angry at Peter for some-such-thing. (Unbeknownst to me) Ann had arranged for Agnes to give Peter a good dose of "medicine" which she was sure Peter wouldn't like.

We were sitting on the sun porch and I could see, Frank, a happy young man with a smiling face, come walking down Manhattan Avenue to our home. I opened the front door for him and, as he stepped inside, I said quite sternly: "I am prepared to pay you fifty cents to take my sister to the movies." His eyes flew wide with shock as he said, "But, we have a date. I'm already taking her to the movies."

As you may have surmised, Ann stifled her hysteria and Agnes flashed me a look that said, "You'll hear about this later!" And, you can believe I did--in the most articulate and reprimanding way. Had I known anything about their "plan," I wouldn't have said a word. But, that didn't matter to Agnes. I had committed an unpardonable *sin.*

Another Sunday afternoon date brought a handsome and polite young man who took Agnes to a movie in Englewood. I think those "dates" were designed to tweak Peter because they had broken off "going steady," something our Mother knew nothing about.

When Agnes and her date came home, he took note of me sitting in the rocker in the living room. In a soft, polite tone, he said, "The eternal triangle." I took the hint and joined Mom in the kitchen for tea.

Whether those dates ever did "tweak" Peter continues to be a mystery to me. He seemed always to be nearby whenever we went to the movies. We'd enter the auditorium by the right aisle, going about three-quarters of the way down and, even in the dark, Agnes would elbow me and say, "Did you see who's sitting in the back?"

"Where," I asked, turning around

She yanked my arm. "You don't have to turn around!"

"I had to turn around to see who you were asking about, Agnes." I followed her into the row of seats.

"If you had to ask who I was talking about, then you didn't see who I was talking about, did you?"

"No."

"Then, all you had to say was, *no*." Her logic always made so much sense and, somehow, made me feel so inept. But, she was right, as usual. The last thing she wanted was to make it obvious that she had seen Peter which, of course, I didn't quite get at the time.

Part Three

The 1940s

As the calendar turned a new decade, the U.S. population was approximately 132,122,000. The minimum wage was raised to forty-three cents per hour, yet the average salary remained around $1,299 per year. The People listened to *Bewitched, Bothered, and Bewildered*; they didn't accept the *bewitched* part, but the *bothered* and *bewildered* seemed more akin to their real feelings.

World War I had been called "the War to end all wars"-- it wasn't. The motion pictures and songs produced for public consumption during the 1930s were all too obvious, despite the popular tune *It's a Big, Wide Wonderful World.* How could anyone really believe that? Hitler had already seized Poland; there weren't many who believed that he didn't have his sights keenly focused on the rest of the continent. *Mein Kampf* made clear his objectives.

I remember so well our Dad telling us, "It's a rich man's war, and a poor boys fight." He said it was a quote associated with the Civil War and never did he ever change his mind, even when Lyndon Johnson committed our young men to VietNam.

World War II was the antidote for the *Great* Depression, its far-reaching impact still being felt all these sixty-four years later. I can't help but believe that the War served as a catalyst for the slow and insidious decline of womanhood. The men who went off to war weren't thinking or fantasizing about *Rosie the Riveter*, it was the likes of Betty Grable and Lana Turner who put American soldiers *In the Mood* and dreaming of home.

England's demands made possible wages the likes of which the People had never seen in any previous decades. With higher wages came higher prices and rationing--both of which occurred in rapid succession.

We all continued in the frugality of our lives, walking to church on Sunday mornings, then to Moe Lieberman's for our Sunday papers, and then, to the bakery for our danish or coffee cake after Sunday dinner. Our Mother prepared breakfast as she always had, and we read the newspapers and listened to the radio.

After December 7, 1941 we prayed for all our men who were fighting and dying in far off lands. And I, as every other American, remember that Sunday and exactly what I was doing when I first learned that the Japanese had bombed our fleet at Pearl Harbor.

The decade of the 1940s for Father Coughlin began with his "official" return to his parish. The Vatican had censored *The Radio Priest* whose broadcasts garnered larger listening audiences than had Roosevelt's. I didn't understand why the Vatican had purged Father Coughlin, who only confirmed what the People already knew; their savings were gone, doctors, police, and firemen were impossible to find, and conditions in the country had not gotten any better, as FDR had promised. We were headed for war--which the People most definitely didn't want.

Our parents had experienced the pre- and post-World War I era. There they were, twenty years later, seeing the prelude to yet another war. They listened to the talk against Roosevelt and the rumors that he, Churchill, and Stalin had planned World War II. After all, what had any one of the three of them to lose? Their countries--in fact, the whole world--were still in the grips of the Depression. For those who had a job, their wages could only be classified as subsistence. War was the unavoidable cure-all. At eighteen, even I saw the handwriting on the wall.

Our Mother's view was: "We're a free country and entitled to a better life, but going to war isn't the way to achieve either." Agnes believed that: "We don't need to get involved in a war and send our boys thousands of miles away to fight for people who won't fight their own battles." But, isn't that how it has always been?

We were (and remained) as patriotic as the next American. It was terribly difficult not to see the greed of the very few at the pinnacle of power who used those beneath them to pickup the tab and provide the blood.

During the war years, Agnes answered all the letters from the young men with whom she had gone to school, and those she had dated.

(Somewhere there's a footlocker with all those wartime letters from young men who served in every branch of service from Europe to the Pacific, and in between.) They had danced to Glenn Miller's *Moonlight Serenade,* and *Careless*, and understood the danger they faced as Frank Sinatra sang, *I'll Never Smile Again*, wondering if they'd survive the horror of war when it came.

I often thought about Franklin Roosevelt's (in)famous speech in which he said: *"I have seen war... your boys will not go off to war."* I'm sure he also sang, *Hi-Diddle-Dee*, the war has turned for me!

We ventured into Manhattan on a regular basis to attend Novena services and to shop the stores. With today's societal concerns, it seems inconceivable to think that two teenage girls would travel into New York City without fear of any harm coming to them. The truth is, people respected the law and the lives of others. God knows it was hard enough to survive without having to worry about the consequences of illegal acts. One might as well stop breathing for things to have been worse than they were. Crime was left to the gangsters and their followers.

Our excursions into Manhattan were memorable; sometimes we would venture down to the Diamond District and occasionally, we'd go to the Shrine of Mother Cabrini in The Bronx, on St. Nicholas Avenue in Upper Manhattan. We always made certain that we stopped for our favorite sandwich of cream cheese on whole wheat raisin bread, and a hot cup of coffee.

Radio brought us such wonderful talent, Arthur Godfrey and Red Skelton, and the two I liked the best, Abbott and Costello. Hollywood churned out movies we either saw at the theaters in Englewood or in Passaic; or at the Paramount, Roxy, or State Theaters in Manhattan.

Walking into the Paramount Theater was an experience in itself. White marble columns elegantly reached for the lobby ceiling as a magnificent staircase wound skyward to the balcony, and the thousands of seats inside the auditorium. Gilted ceilings glistened with the myriad of lights from the crystal chandelier as if announcing its anticipation of royalty. The lighting mellowed the lush, red velvet drapes and red carpeting below as brightly polished brass rails constrained the theatergoers in the majesty of their surroundings. Even the *Powder Room* continued the grand sense of elegance. At some point we learned that the Paramount had been designed in the fashion of the Paris Opera House.

Under the Hays Office, wholesome movies were the order of the day, and no one--not even the Courts--forced the issue of *free speech.* No one claimed the "right" to produce pornography or to verbalize obscenities as has been done since the 1960s when the Hays Code was abandoned. "Romance" in motion pictures and in song was portrayed in all of its charm and innocence; and what followed it was left entirely to one's imagination, unlike today, where nothing is left to anyone's imagination.

The young men Agnes and I dated wouldn't dare make improper advances or they'd get their faces slapped. I can honestly say that the young men of our day were so very different, but then so, too, were the young women.

A young man's limit of *unseemliness* was whistling or yelling out to a girl who, quite respectably, ignored him. Inwardly, she might be thrilled that the boy had noticed and made his feelings known; but it was the *rare occasion* when the girl responded to such daring behavior. To do so would result in her being labeled *fast and loose* which was the kiss of death in a small town.

Penicillin, income tax withholding, the GI Bill, the Cold War, Communist "Red" China, the State of Israel, the Middle East's near-exclusivity over oil distribution, and the United Nations, were but a few of the *bi-products* of the 1940s.

Ultimately, the War eliminated America's isolationist agenda, Constitutional provisions for the collection of taxes, and countless millions of lives, leaving untold millions more to forever mourn their lost loved ones.

On the socio-economic side, the *Great* Depression had all but ended the manipulation of the world's masses. Those who survived the Depression were left to question (and curse) those whose machinations went far beyond the Depression.

1940

Unemployment was reported at 14.6%; our National Debt at $50.7-Billion, and Federal Spending at a *mere* $9.47-Billion.

Few people took serious note of Congress' refusal to renew its trade treaty with Japan, or that our Country was implementing an air defense program against a *possible attack.* In hindsight, the timeline of events suggests that while World War II hadn't yet begun for us, America was already "unofficially" at war.

People seemed fixated with the news that the first Social Security checks were going to be sent out, while FDR asked Congress for $1.3-Billion in supplemental funding for military and naval development. People heard the tune, *I Haven't Time to Be a Millionaire*, because they were too busy being broke.

Hattie McDaniel became the first African American to receive an Academy Award for her portrayal as Scarlett's "Mammy" in David O. Selznick's production of *Gone With The Wind.*

Agnes and I and our girlfriends continued our occasional afternoon walks over the Seven Sisters to the Palisades as they sang the *Ferry Boat Serenade.* They harmonized so well, singing one popular tune after another. They made the trip seem shorter than it was for, suddenly, we were overlooking the Hudson River.

It was the spring of 1940 and two of the popular songs at all of our high school dances were, *Dolores* and *Polka Dots and Moonbeams.* Later that summer, Frank Sinatra's *I'll Never Smile Again*, stole the top spot on the charts.

Agnes was sixteen (and a half) and a boy named Bill took her to an early evening show to see Frank Sinatra at the Paramount in Manhattan. Afterwards, they went to *Lindy's* for a slice of their famous cheesecake. It was a pretty "big-time" date, so to speak, and I remember how totally spellbound Agnes was with the song and with Frank Sinatra. She had gone on for over an hour describing the handsome, yet skinny, young crooner.

I found my first *real* job as a sales girl at Burnt's Bakery on West Englewood Avenue in West Englewood. (I don't recall whether I had seen an advertisement in the newspaper or if I had placed one.) The owners were two very kindhearted Germans who had owned the bakery for several years. The husband often reminisced about his days as a soldier in World War I and spoke of his disappointment with Hitler and how he had stolen power from the people which, Mr. Burnt had said, the people were incapable of stopping.

Newspapers, magazines, and radio broadcasts were filled with stories about Hitler, while theater newsreels provided the visual side of the German people who seemed quite happy with their new socialist leader.

At the end of my first month at the bakery, Mr. Burnt called me aside and said, "You keep everything so nice and clean. Mrs. Burnt is very satisfied with you, so I am going to raise your pay by a dime." Instead of the twenty-five cents an hour that he had agreed to pay me, I would now be earning thirty-five cents an hour for my seven-hour shift from 7:30 a.m. to 2:30 p.m. The couple also said that I could have my choice of a very nice dessert and a loaf of bread each day when I left work. Luckily, walking to and from work every day helped burn all those delicious calories!

During the Depression years, nearly everybody walked, even to the few bus stops that were sometimes miles apart. Those who finally had a little more money in their pockets were able to purchase gasoline for their automobiles (if they still had one).

As I walked home from work, I remember the many times that Ann met me as I turned onto Manhattan Avenue. "C'mon in, let's have some tea." (I had the dessert!) Her excitement gushed as she told me about Carlo, the young fellow she was dating that year. She told me he was in the construction business with his father and drove a brand new 1940 red Ford Convertible. He paid six-hundred-dollars, as she told me. (Today, we can't even buy a set of tires for that price!)

Agnes was maturing, punctuated by a fiery temper that made things *interesting*. At the end of the mid-term, she and her gym teacher had a "confrontation."

"She was entirely out of line," Agnes said.

"What did she say," we all asked her at the supper table.

"That my art wasn't going to get me a passing grade in gym--unless I sketched her portrait! So, I threw my book at her and walked out."

Agnes wanted to quit school then and there, but our parents would hear no such thing. They decided that she would go full-time (during the summer) for private art instruction which her teachers had continually encouraged our parents to do throughout her school years. She was always being chosen to design the yearbook covers, as well as the displays for various class projects. What Agnes didn't know was that our parents had already decided--she was going to remain in school.

What isn't often mentioned about those years is that the Depression had caused many schools to close and teenagers were leaving school upon reaching their sixteenth birthdays. But I had stayed the course--and so would Agnes.

One would had to have been blind not to see the sensitivity in her art. She was her happiest when drawing, or painting, or whittling on a bar of soap. Her talent, good looks, and all the attention she got could have made her very conceited and arrogant, but she wasn't in the least. The attention only made her all the more humble and shy, which seemed to intrigue the boys who vied for her attention. I was proud to have such a pretty and talented sister.

During those summer months, Agnes slept a little later than I who left for work at 7:00 a.m. I recall, as I dressed for work one morning, that I was humming *A Nightingale Sang in Barkley Square*. Now, I wasn't the type to sing, and rarely did I hum but, for some reason, I was in a happy mood that morning. (It could have been payday for all I remember.)

Agnes called out, "I can hear you, Margaret!" then rolled over and buried her head under the pillow. She took her sleep seriously, preferring to stay up later in the evenings doing her sketches for art class.

She spent four hours each day with the instructors, then came home and did whatever housework had to be done. When Mom, Dad, and I returned at the end of the work day, the house was spotless and smelling of the incense we bought during our Saturday shopping trips and which put the final touch on her meticulous cleaning.

Sometimes, after her art lessons, Agnes would walk to the bakery to meet me, and then we would join up with some of our friends and go *looking* in the stores, or stop in the music shop to listen to the latest tunes. We spent hours seriously considering the songs we absolutely had to have in our record collections.

One of the stories Agnes always loved to tell was about one afternoon in June that she had come to the bakery to walk home with me. I had selected a loaf of fresh-baked bread and especially recall the chocolate pie with its high mound of whipped cream on top. I handed Agnes the loaf of bread and we walked along West Englewood Avenue, enjoying the beauty of the early summer day. As we approached the curb at State Street, suddenly, down I went. The box with the chocolate pie sailed into the air and landed upside down next to me on the pavement.

Agnes wasn't laughing. She stood poised, looking distantly across the street, and calmly said, "Get up, you're embarrassing me!" It's very telling of the young lady's pride and who forever thought I should have been a little more patient--and observant.

A good many of our walks were memorable as was the afternoon Christy, the tall, good-looking young fellow with dark hair, seized yet another opportunity to tease me. We were passing the Monument in Englewood and Christy yelled out, "Hey, Agnes! Why don't you send your chaperone home?!" He was known for his high-decibel yelling--whether across the street, next to you, or on the telephone. He called Agnes one day and I heard his voice clear across the living room. I didn't have to look up to see that she was holding the receiver a full arm's length away from her ear.

Christy worked with Sam, the young man I was dating at the time, who was employed as a neon sign designer in Hackensack.

That June brought the passage of the Conscription Bill and I remember arguing with our friend, Ann, that FDR must have been behind it. She followed the news a bit more meticulously than I and defended FDR, insisting that it had been two *Republicans*, named Wadsworth and Burke, who had successfully gotten *their* Conscription Bill passed. The Selective Service and Training Act required 21-35 year-old men to register for the draft. It also raised taxes and required 5-million aliens to register.

There was a rumor that the new legislation might require *all* citizens to register *if* a draft was called up. I interpreted that reference to "all citizens" to mean the drafting of women as well.

The long, hot summer settled in and, around mid-August, Packy Tiernan, one of our New York cousins started visiting us. He preferred the quiet of the country to the heat of Manhattan. He was the second oldest son of Mom's younger brother and was the most outgoing and fun-loving young man we ever knew. He often brought along a few of his buddies, including a young man, named Jimmy Cummings, who also found the country life a blessed reprieve from the sweltering city.

Jimmy worked for Curtis Publishing on 42nd Street during the day and, in the evenings entertained with his big band--*Jimmy Cummings and His Orchestra*. When he wasn't directing his band, he played the piano. He didn't just *play the piano*, he was truly gifted, but he gave the nuns who taught him most of the credit. Jimmy also wrote many of the songs his band performed when they were booked into some of the Manhattan nightclubs. (He also bore a remarkable resemblance to the Hollywood actor, Robert Walker.)

The boys' visits usually began on Saturday evenings, when they would arrive with a coffee cake or a pie, and Jimmy would have his stack of records that we played for hours on the phonograph. Mom was delighted to have her nephew and his young Irish friends visit. So many wonderful weekends were filled with their laughter and shenanigans. We had a third bedroom upstairs, but our parents made the boys sleep downstairs in the living room or on the sun porch. Propriety and respectability were our parents' orders--which were cast in stone.

Packy, Jimmy, Agnes, and I walked down to one of our favorite haunts, the Englewood Music Store. There was no such thing as having too many records because, invariably, a few of those 78 rpm Victor, Brunswick, or Decca record disks got scratched or broken during the boys' weekend visits.

I remember how the owner of the music store always went out of his way to oblige us, as he did the day Agnes and I asked for the *Hut Sut* song that went: *Hut-Sut Rawlson on the rillerah and a brawla, brawla sooit,* the sassy tune about a town in Sweden that had everyone tapping their toes and wondering what the words really meant.

Peter and Agnes had stopped dating some time in the Spring, and although *Jimmy never ever brought her pretty flowers,* he would make tea for everyone on those sunday mornings before we all walked to church. After services and a late breakfast, Jimmy and Agnes would go see a movie.

The young men would have to leave by eleven p.m. on Sunday night to catch the last "Blue" bus (out of Hackensack) that would take them across the George Washington Bridge for the subway to Park Avenue in mid-Manhattan where Jimmy lived. They avoided Central Park which already had "distinguished" itself for late evening muggings and murders. (I guess some things never change!)

Our cousin Packy, Jimmy Cummings, and their buddies from Manhattan brought a great deal of fun and plenty of laughter whenever they visited. These were such grand times for us all as we approached adulthood.

I was through with school and almost eighteen; I was earning a living and advancing myself. Business school or college was not in the equation, but I was ambitious and knew that if I worked hard, surely, I would amount to something. I just didn't know what kind of work I would be suited to doing.

Agnes got her first part-time job that summer working as a *mother's helper* for a family who lived near Dwight Morrow High School. Our friend, Ann, held the job for a couple of months, but decided to take another position with an elderly lady on Teaneck Road. Ann had come from a large family so, I guess it was fine with her parents that she stayed with the woman who had an illness that kept her home bound. Ann asked Agnes if she'd like to help her with the family and Agnes accepted. Our Mother, however, felt that Agnes should not be working. but, instead be focused on her art, taking care of our home--and finishing school.

By September, nearly 16-million men had registered for the

Draft. On October 16, the Conscription Bill became Federal law. The first number was pulled from a fish bowl which, for me, confirmed that we were going to War. On October 29, the first lottery numbers were pulled in a "fishbowl drawing" selecting the men who would be called to report for military training. It was the first peace time draft and I thought, *Because of You* politicians, more than 16-million men will register for the draft without the *People's* mandate.

Our parents were Democrats. I was soon to be eighteen and, of course, not yet able to register to vote. I would have been in a pickle because I didn't like FDR, but then I wasn't too sure about the Republicans--especially the two who had gotten their Conscription Bill passed. I felt everything our parents had feared was about to happen. All the talk in the country had been against any U.S. involvement in what seemed inevitable. There was no need to draft young men into the military if we weren't going to war, as FDR had promised: *"Your boys will never fight on foreign soil..."* All the signs were before us--Hitler was patiently waiting--and so was FDR.

Fools Rush In was a popular tune that November. I thought the song title quite appropriate--only *fools* could have allowed Roosevelt to break the tradition of a two-term presidency. He seized his opportunity to stamp history with his newfound legacy--though his anti-Depression efforts had all but failed, save Social Security.

Packy and Jimmy registered but, in the meantime, there was too much joy to spread, and Packy planned to have as much fun as God would allow him. I don't think I'll ever forget those Sunday evenings the well-dressed boys from New York--with all the charm to dazzle near-about everyone--left for home singing, *My Gal's a Corker, She's a New Yorker!*

After attending Novena service one evening, Agnes and I stopped into an ice cream parlor for a scoop of vanilla ice cream. I remember tiny black specks in my ice cream and I marched up to the counter man to complain. He politely explained that the "specks" were from the ground-up vanilla beans and offered to let me choose another flavor,. I kept the vanilla--it was one of those youthful learning experiences that Agnes and I laughed about over the years when we'd sit and talk about the many places and things we enjoyed in our youth.

Some time in mid-December, we asked our parents if they would cash-in the insurance policies they had purchased when Agnes and I were a year old. They paid monthly premiums of only ten cents toward policies that could mature to as much as two-hundred dollars. We were thinking about enrolling in beauty school, but only on a part-time basis because Agnes was still in high school, and I had my job at the bakery. Our Mother thought it might be a nice profession for a woman and said that she would call the school on Main Street in Hackensack to make some inquiries and, she would "think about it."

The day the insurance checks arrived, we called our Mother at work to ask if she would let us cash them. She said yes, and we headed off to Jake Rouch's Grocery Store. We brought home the grand sum of one-hundred-thirty dollars which, in those days, was a great deal of money. We put the cash in a Schrafft's lavender-colored candy tin that was beautifully decorated in the Art Nouveau style with a garland of orchid and purple flowers that covered the lid. It measured about seven inches long by four inches wide and three inches high--just perfect for keeping our cash.

I'll admit the money was a temptation, and our Mother gave us permission to take out five dollars--but *only* five dollars--not a penny more, and we were very pleased.

We went into Manhattan to the Paramount Theater that December afternoon. I don't recall the movie, but Ray Herbeck and his Orchestra was the featured band. Henny Youngman was the comic, along with the singing group, the Ink Spots. My mind is filled with the vision of that unforgettable show...

The house lights dimmed to black as a warming glow came from above and a brilliant spotlight beamed down on the stage that slowly ascended from the level of the orchestra pit. We heard the voices of the four men before we saw them standing in bright white suits, singing, *We Three...we're all alone...*" That song became one of the Ink Spots' greatest hits. We had seen the group the year before, but that night's performance left an indelible impression as no other since that evening.

Whenever we reminisced about the countless trips we had made into Manhattan to see the Big Bands, that December afternoon remained as clear (and alive) as if it were happening before our eyes when we were young.

We saw the newsreel of the day, followed by the main feature, and afterwards, we went for our usual treat: the sandwich with a heaping wedge of cream cheese on whole wheat raisin bread and a hot cup of Chockful O'Nuts coffee. (It's where I acquired my taste for coffee.) The sandwich was a dime and the coffee a nickel--what a bargain. Today, a cup of coffee is around two dollars, and I have to wonder *how* a cup of coffee got so damned expensive!

Occasionally, we went to the State Theater in Manhattan to see a first-run film and a band, or we'd buy tickets to the Roxy Theater which also featured first-run films, along with their famous dance troupe, the *Rockettes*.

The Paramount had represented the glamour of old Europe and so, too, did the Roxy. A huge reception area, filled with dozens of ushers, held the crowds at bay until the ushers directed them to the staircase that led to the balcony, or to the lobby's huge set of ornate doors that provided access to the rotunda of the theater, the orchestra pit, and the loge seating areas. Magnificent columns framed windows from on high in an auditorium as deep as it was wide. Seven or eight aisles divided the wide span of seats which had to be in the thousands. In the center of the balcony was a deep recess that housed the projection equipment.

If we attended a matinee, there was always time to go to

Woolworth's 5 & 10 Cent Store near 42nd Street. Their unequaled selection of makeup, combs, perfumes, hair ribbons, and the like held us captive for hours. As we approached 1941, a very popular style for women with longer hair came into vogue. A comb with a pretty colored ribbon attached was positioned to hold a cluster of curls at the top of one's head. I used the comb style more than Agnes who didn't particularly like the fad.

Oftentimes, we would catch a subway to 34th Street where Gimbels and Macy's department stores stood since opening their doors at the turn-of-the-century. If we had a little extra money, you can be sure that shopping was held to necessities, not anything frivolous.

Christmas came and we celebrated it as we had all the previous years, except that we weren't children anymore. We were responsible young ladies now.

Our Dad worked the midnight to eight a.m. shift that New Year's Eve. Mom, Agnes and I sat listening to Guy Lombardo who, each year, broadcast from the Waldorf Astoria Hotel in New York City.

After a day of food preparation and house cleaning for the holiday, we were still wide awake and full of energy as Guy Lombardo's band played "*Auld Lang Syne.*"

"We're going to tidy-up the house," Agnes said.

Mom shrugged her shoulders. "Yer goin' to *clean* the already cleaned house," she said through a smiled. "Just be sure ye turn off the radio before ye go up to bed."

We both had helped Mom prepare the food for New Year's dinner, along with some baked goods and we did all the general cleaning. I had polished the stairs that morning, rubbing the hard paste wax onto the exposed pine on both sides of the carpeted runner and Agnes had dusted all of the furniture and knickknacks in the living and dining rooms and set the round oak table for dinner. There really wasn't anything left to do.

I think we finally gave in and went up to bed a few hours later. Dad came home around seven in the morning; we went to Mass New Year's Day, returned with our favorite newspapers, had dinner, and listened to the radio.

1941

Federal Spending was recorded at $13.65-Billion, the Federal Debt at $57.5-Billion, and unemployment was reported at 9.9%.

Glenn Miller's *Chattanooga Choo-Choo* was the rage, and the *Screwtape Letters,* by C.S. Lewis, arrived in the Country's book stores. Agnes read the book and even drew her interpretations of the Lewis characters. She sketched one with the head of Franklin Roosevelt sitting in his office with her caption: *Oh, Look at Me Now*.

Cousin Packy and Jimmy continued their occasional weekend visits and the talk of war went on as Hitler's Third Reich crushed one European country after another. In February, the Nazis installed their Vichy government in France, while Hitler's General Rommel led his steel-helmeted soldiers into Tripoli on the North African continent. Bob Hope and Bing Crosby's *Road to Zanzibar* provided comic relief for the People.

In March, Roosevelt got his Lend-Lease program, which allowed him to ship American-made war materiel to England and to the Soviet Union. The People didn't know when, or where, or how we would be drawn into the war, they just knew it was inevitable, and only a matter of time.

Before the end of May, word came that the German battleship *Bismarck* had been sunk. It was a major victory for England, and *The White Cliffs of Dover* played more frequently on the radio. For us, the

Jersey Bounce became a favorite with our group of four as we continued our treks up the Seven Sisters to the Palisades while Agnes and the other girls sang, *I'll Be With You in Apple Blossom Time*. They weren't the Andrews Sisters, but then, no one had any problem recognizing the tune.

We were well aware that war was raging in Europe and England was being bombed by Hitler's Luftwaffe, but we felt the war was *over there*. By the end of June, everyone had heard that the little "paperhanger's" Nazi troops were marching into the Soviet Union, still a world away.

As Summer approached, we were dating two young artists who came into favor because of Agnes' art classes. One was a tall dark-haired fellow named Ken, and the other shorter fellow with brown hair, named Vic.

The young men came one evening to pick us up for a date. We sat in the living room, trying to decide whether to go to the pizza parlor with a dance floor, or to a movie. They began talking about art, asked Agnes about her training, and spoke of the importance of knowing human anatomy. Ken said, "All figure sketching and painting begins with the *nude*." Vic said he was particularly fond of the nudes Italian artist Angelo Asti had drawn.

I looked at Agnes and she looked at me. I immediately understood the look in her eyes, while she dropped her gaze to the floor. I stood up, walked to the French doors at the sun porch, and said, "It was nice of you both to stop by, but it's time for you to go." They looked quite surprised, hesitating to ask *why* they were being asked to leave. "Yes, I agree. The visit is over," Agnes said and walked to the kitchen.

Back then, there was never any doubt about the Peoples' attitude regarding the "proper" things that could be discussed, and the "improper" things that should *never* be discussed. While both young men were artists, and their conversation addressed art, the subject of *nudes* was totally inappropriate. (We were daring enough to travel into the big city, but so terribly innocent and "unsophisticated" that we wouldn't even consider the *impertinent* conversation! Today, of course, not only do young peoples' conversations cover vastly more revealing subjects, but their actions, as well.)

One afternoon in June, we received a phone call from a young lady, named Connie. She introduced herself and said that she, along with her brother and father, had just moved into the neighborhood and bought a house on Washington Place. (The house previously owned by the German family whose son allowed Agnes to "fly" his bi-plane). Connie said that she would like to come over and meet us because we were all close in age.

We sat in the lawn chairs next to the house and she told us that her father was a "G-Man."

"Oh! He works for the government," I said.

"No, he's a garbage man. We have three trucks," she said, and explained that she did the bookkeeping, her brother ran the office in their home, and her father supervised the waste management crews who drove their trucks.

Agnes thought Connie was a real character, with a capital "C," but a nice one who had a great sense of humor. She told Connie that since her father was a "G-Man" she better not get caught listening to *Truth Or Consequences*, the new game show on the radio.

"Oh, I always tell the truth, no matter how bad it is," Connie said.

Agnes smiled. "And, how do you take the consequences?"

"Usually with coffee and a piece of cake!" That was Connie, always turning a joke. No matter how serious a situation, Connie always managed to make you laugh. Our friendship lasted over twenty years.

We discussed my job and Connie said that because her father provided his service to nearly all of the businesses in Englewood, she was always hearing about job openings and mentioned one such opening with Leonard's Ladies Clothing Company. She said she would introduce me to the manager. Connie asked if he would give Agnes and me a discount on the clothes we purchased, which he said he would.

Nearly all of our friends had either part- or full-time jobs. Agnes didn't see why she shouldn't have one, too. She had earned all of the necessary credits to receive her diploma at the end of the school term the following June. She focused her attention on her art and decided that she was ready for a part-time job.

Unbeknownst to our parents, she applied and was hired as a waitress trainee at the Mary Elizabeth Tea Room in Englewood. It was an upscale establishment and catered to the society folks from the Englewood Cliffs, including several entertainers who settled in the Jersey countryside.

The Mary Elizabeth Tea Room was a forerunner of our modern-day *bed and breakfast* establishments. It was a very elegant 1880s Victorian home which the owner, a sixty-year-old lady, had purchased years earlier. She interviewed Agnes, hired her, and provided the black rayon dress with a matching lacey head piece, along with a bib apron and white shoes. To the *stuffy* lady's way of thinking, it was a *privilege* to be seen at her establishment--even as a trainee.

Agnes came home late one afternoon and announced that she had spilled a glass of ice water all over Carmen Cavallero, the internationally-known society pianist. It didn't sit well with our Mother. Agnes quit two days later--at our Mother's urging who thought she could do better than serving glasses of ice water and baskets of bread. "Had I known ye were going to apply for it, I never would have allowed it," she said.

The heat of August embroiled us, and our Mother was in an

uproar after reading in her Catholic newspapers that Hitler had ordered the killing of the handicapped and those with mental disorders. "He's a demon out of hell," she said. It was a shocking revelation to think that anyone would deliberately kill those who were as children, with no control over their handicap or mental disorder. (When the Terri Schiavo case came to light in Florida, I thought of what our Mother would have to say about the same thinking which, obviously, has begun to take hold in America.)

I gave Mr. Burnt notice that I was resigning, however, I didn't take the sales position that Connie had arranged. I interviewed for receptionist position with the Marcus Decorating and Upholstery Shop, also in Englewood.

It was a job I nearly lost, after only two months, when one of the company delivery men brought me three pairs of stockings--at a time when stockings were scarce and very expensive. I refused his offer, but he left them on my desk anyway. I told my Mother and showed her the box. She snatched it out of my hands, said she would "take care of it," and huffed out of the house.

She returned a half hour later and gave me a full account: she went to the man's home, knocked on the door, and told his wife that she wanted to speak with the man who had given her young daughter three pairs of stockings.

"If ye ever go near my daughter again or hold a conversation with her, I'll break yer damn neck! I ought to break it fer ye now and be done with it!" she had said.

I thought, *He'll tell the owner for sure.*

"He'll not be botherin' ye again, Margaret," she said, nodding her head. "I've taken care of it!." Her parting words to his wife were: "Keep yer dirty thing at home!"

Oh, Lord, there goes my job!

Years later, I thought about that incident and realized that the man had meant no harm, it was an innocent gesture, yet my Mother considered it entirely inappropriate. There was no in-between with her; the *appearance* of things was to be guarded at all times.

Agnes informed us that she had applied at the Plaza Theater to become an usherette. One of the perks was free admission for family members.

The nice thing about small home towns is that no one is a stranger and our Dad stopped by the Plaza to talk with Marie who, for years, had been the head cashier. She assured him that the usherette position was good employment for a young lady and that there were special requirements for usherettes--for ushers, as well, (until Pearl Harbor, when the ushers who had gone off to war were replaced with usherettes.) The young usherettes were required to wear uniforms; dark Navy blue dresses with gold braiding and belt, a white ruffled blouse, along with a small round pillbox hat, stockings, and mid-heeled shoes. They carried flashlights to guide patrons to their seats in the darkened theater.

Mr. Kerry, the theater manager, was a very professional and polite man who treated his employees fairly and with considerable respect. The "trend" was toward hiring young women because the draft had begun removing men from the workplace.

Agnes got the job and, as each usherette was occasionally required to do, reported for work early in the mornings, three days each week to cover phone duty. Those mornings allowed for a lunch break at eleven and then the usherettes reported for their 4:30 p.m. shift. One evening, Agnes told us that she had stopped into St. Cecelia's Church and was standing at the heater unit in the vestibule before going for lunch. A nun came up and reprimanded her, "Get back to your class!"

Agnes spent the better part of her lunch hour trying to convince the nun that she didn't go to school and was working at the theater downtown.

My sister was the driving force behind two of the other usherettes who asked Mr. Kerry if they could decorate the three small dressing rooms behind the stage; making it easier to change into their uniforms before and after their shifts. She was only a humble little usherette in the middle of a hometown theatrical environment, but it was sufficient to spark her interest in costume design and set decoration, which she became involved with in later years.

"Confidence" should have been Agnes' middle name. She told me how the head usherette had cried when Mr. Kerry asked her to go into Manhattan to pick up the lobby cards (advertising posters that promoted the upcoming movies). He tried to assure her it was perfectly safe and would not take any more time than the bus trip from Englewood to 168th Street for the "A" train to 42nd Street and Broadway. Add only a few minutes to pick-up the lobby cards, and then make the return trip back to Englewood.

"You should have seen the way she cried, Margaret. She said she'd never been to New York City alone and it was too far to go alone," Agnes said. "Mr. Kerry didn't know what to do when the other usherettes also declined because they were too frightened to go into the city alone."

"And, let me guess--*you,* the youngest of all the usherettes, volunteered," I said.

"Well, of course! Skorous' main office is right near the Church of the Holy Cross on 42nd Street," she said. "Mr. Kerry is going to pay my hourly wages *and* reimburse my expenses going into and coming back from Manhattan!"

"*And*, naturally, once you're in the city, you can always stop into some of the stores downtown."

She laughed. "You know me so well!"

Agnes took a genuine interest in everything--which is probably why Mr. Kerry allowed his newly-employed usherette to assume the *weekly* responsibility to travel to their Broadway office.

We had seen Peter in town on occasion, but Agnes and he still weren't dating. I didn't ask why, because I knew Agnes wouldn't tell. She was a very private person not given to complaining or gossiping.

There was one event that Fall, in early November which puzzled me. Two years earlier, Roosevelt had designated the *third* Thursday as the *official* day the Country would celebrate Thanksgiving. However, that November 1941, he changed the date again, *back* to the *fourth* Thursday. I don't recall ever hearing any explanation for the date change.

A week after thanking God for our blessings and not being involved in the War, came December 7, 1941. It's a date I remember so well, as has every soul alive on that day never forgetting where they were and what they were doing that early winter Sunday...

Agnes and I had gone to the nine o'clock Mass and returned home to have breakfast with our parents. Connie and her cousin Louise from Jersey City, came over to join me in walking Agnes down to the Plaza Theater for her two o'clock shift and then we'd stay to see the feature film.

It was a bright, sunny December day and we hadn't a hint of what was happening nearly six-thousand miles away in Honolulu, Hawaii. We arrived at the theater around one o'clock and Connie, Louise, and I took our seats to see the main feature, *Dr. Jekyll and Mr. Hyde,* with Spencer Tracy, Ingrid Bergman, and Lana Turner. Midway through the film, suddenly, the screen went black. The two side curtains slowly closed, meeting each other in the center. The house lights came up and Mr. Kerry walked across the darkened stage with the spotlight focused on him.

He spoke calmly and with authority: "All servicemen are to report to their units immediately. The Japanese have bombed our naval base at Pearl Harbor, in Hawaii."

Roosevelt's Executive Order required all men whose draft numbers had been selected in the autumn of 1940 to report for duty immediately. Several young men--some in uniform and some who were not, those with young ladies and those without--quietly got up and left the theater.

The doorman, an elderly gentleman, consoled Agnes who was in tears at the thought of all the young men who were going to be sent off to war. The old gent explained, as a veteran of World War I, that's not what immediately happens and it would be several days or weeks before the men would be sent anywhere. Their first destinations would be to boot camp for training.

Agnes' shift ended around six-thirty when the usherettes for the evening schedule arrived. We all walked home to find our parents fixed at the radio listening to the news of the bombing.

Mom said, "All the young men whose lives were lost today, and those who will be lost...Heaven's gate will be opened to their souls; and for those who have caused this War--Hell will be waiting..." Dad said, "The fat cats will make millions of dollars off this war--at the cost of millions of lives sacrificed."

The banner headline in Monday morning's paper read: *WAR DECLARED!* That Monday, December 8, brought FDR's (in)famous radio address about that *Day in Infamy*. He had asked Congress for a Declaration of War against Japan and the axis powers of Germany and Italy.

America was at War.

I was furious, feeling that Roosevelt had lied about "*not wanting to send your boys off to war*," and I thought about the rush to draft our men. I thought about all the factories that had geared-up to provide England and the Soviet Union with all kinds of war munitions, and supplies. Now those factories would be running twenty-four hours a day.

The week following Pearl Harbor, Agnes and I double-dated with two young men, Freddie and Charlie. Freddie introduced himself to Agnes at the Plaza Theater when he went to see Mr. Kerry to discuss the theater's needs for heating oil. I remember how Agnes and I stood at the bedroom window looking out at the snow-covered drive as the young men drove down Manhattan Avenue. Rarely would we be waiting in the living room; it wasn't proper "to be waiting."

They took us to the Capital Theater in Passaic to see the musical, *Blues in the Night,* along with Vaughn Monroe who sang his memorable song, *There I Go*, with his orchestra accompanying him.

Freddie came along with Charlie, who drove his Dad's 1938 black Cadillac. They were taking us to dinner in Chinatown and then, to Times Square to celebrate New Year's Eve.

There wasn't room enough for feet on the street with the thousands who had crowded into Times Square. Men and women of every age and mothers and fathers with children filled the world's most famous setting as America faced the unknown that would come with 1942.

No one showed any outward signs of feeling the cold of that winter's night; the herd of revelers refused to be intimidated, or to be held captive to any thing or person, save Father Time who stole the remaining moments of 1941.

Agnes and I wore white silk blouses in different designs; black skirts, silk stockings with black high-heeled shoes, and tailored black wool crepe coats designed in the Princess style.

Charlie maneuvered us through the crush of celebrants and, finally, reached the George Washington Bridge. Our Mother greeted us at the door and both Freddie and Charlie wished her a Happy New Year.

"And, the same to ye both," she said with a smile, looking at her wristwatch. It was two a.m., her extended curfew hour for New Year's Eve. The three of us sat in the kitchen with our cups of hot tea talking for another hour.

1942

Federal Spending was reported at $35.14-Billion, with a Federal Debt of $79.2-Billion. *But*, unemployment dropped to 4.7%, the lowest in the thirteen years of the *Great* Depression, and the Country sang, *At Last*.

Glenn Miller served up *Moonlight Cocktails* as Roosevelt and his generals divined their war plans under America's Declaration of War--effectively telling our boys: *Put Your Dreams Away* for another day, *This is the Army, Mr. Jones*.

Hollywood and Broadway stars joined the war effort to raise everyone's morale as the Country's young danced to *I Left My Heart at the Stage Door Canteen... Who Wouldn't Love You... I've Got a Gal In Kalamazoo...* and *I'll Be Around*.

The composers of the 1940s wrote songs that lifted the spirits, if only temporarily. Other songs seemed to wrap those on the home front in a haunting reverie for loved ones in some far off theater of battle.

The War, ever on our minds, brought us to a semi-dream state of the here and now. Surviving was the overwhelming task of the day in suspended reality--which Hollywood obliged. Celebrities appeared at war bond rallies and at USO canteens around the country. And, *Thanks for the Memories*, Bob Hope, for making our boys' lives an hour or two happier through humor, song, and memories of home.

It may seem unfathomable to today's generation to know that the entire Country had come together to stand behind not only our troops and the war, but behind the Commander-in-Chief, even for those (like me) who didn't like or support Roosevelt. Despite the rumors of collusion about those who wanted us in the war, inspite of rampant suspicions that the war was the "means to an end," the Country stood firm. Politicians on both sides of the aisle held their rhetoric, dispensing with political vitriol and partisan quislingism, or giving tacit "aid and comfort" to our enemies, which everyone knew back then was *Treason*. That word, along with so many others, no longer has meaning or value, in a new and bastardized vocabulary.

As technologically deprived as we were, without the benefit of instantaneous news reporting; as financially beleaguered as the People were for over a decade, God and Country were the mainstays of our sanity and survival.

Having lost the reverence due God, our Country seems to have spiraled into a black hole of nihilism. My generation was rich in faith, cradled in hope and charity, and confident that right and justice would prevail in the end--and most of the time it did.

The United States began broadcasting news of the War over *Voice of America* to Europeans trapped by the axis powers. *Tokyo Rose* spread her own propaganda to our boys caught on Bataan and Corregidor in the Pacific.

Daylight Saving Time went into effect, primarily to conserve energy and, while the Conscription Bill hadn't succeeded in drafting women, Roosevelt signed a Bill establishing the WAACs--the Women's Auxiliary Army Corps.

Patriotism and fear represented the dichotomy of our lives as *our* War got under way. Air Raid Wardens and Block Leaders were put in place to monitor the landscape on behalf of the civilian war effort, knocking on doors if lights could be seen through house windows. Automobile headlamps were altered with plates that restricted the flood of light to narrow rectangular slits; and armed soldiers guarding the bridges over the Hudson and Passaic Rivers became the norm as our lives changed in ways we couldn't have anticipated.

Air raid sirens blared and, in spite of it all, we clung to the sense that we would be safe; even when Agnes and I were caught in a Manhattan subway, in a tunnel beneath thousands of tons of concrete and asphalt, during one of those air raids.

There was a small Army camp north of Englewood in Orangeburg. It was off the Knickerbocker and Shalenburg Roads, just over the New Jersey state line, on the New York side. From it ran that familiar brown bus filled with soldiers who came into Englewood on weekend passes, or those who were being transported to the docks along the Hudson River to board ships for unknown destinations.

Our family physician, Dr. Jordan was on the local draft board as the examining physician. I remember him telling our Mother, "It sometimes makes your heart sink that so many of these young men need dental work and their health isn't as it should be; having been deprived of good nourishment during the depression years..." Mom was terribly sad hearing this which only made us all feel that much worse for our young men going off to war.

Valentine's Day brought Jimmy Cummings and His Orchestra to Englewood for a dance. He opened with his theme song, *Don't Blame Me,* and then introduced his own originally-written tune, *The Englewood Jump,* which puffed the party celebrants' chests with pride. Jimmy had written for them their own answer to Benny Goodman's popular *Jersey Bounce*. I sat stage right with Agnes, finally seeing Jimmy Cummings and his Orchestra perform after hearing so much about his big band.

In March, Freddie and Charlie missed picking us up at the appointed time for our dates. Freddie and Charlie called, and Charlie explained that his father had asked him to work a later shift in their oil distribution company and would come later--if that was okay.

"No, it isn't okay," Agnes said. "When someone makes an appointment with us, we expect it to be kept. Tell your father to keep you busy for the rest of your evenings because you won't be coming back here." We joked that the two of them were probably singing *Blues in the Night* after *that* phone call.

A week later, I received a letter from Charlie, asking if because Agnes and Freddie had broken up, did that mean *we also wouldn't be seeing each other.* I didn't answer his letter. However, he sent several more letters, then came to see me one evening before he was shipped overseas. He brought an engagement ring. I liked Charlie, but not enough to marry him--I was seeing Sam. And, if I hadn't been dating Sam, my answer would have been the same.

Engagement and marriage were entered into by two people who, though attracted to each other, were making a lifelong commitment during a time in which no one knew if the young man would ever return. The young soldiers wanted someone back home to write to and know that their "special someone" was thinking and praying for them.

Too often, reality reared its ugly head--some of the young women who had promised "commitment" were too impatient to wait for their new husbands, and the "Dear John" letters went out. How devastating it must have been for those young men whose lives were so expendable and in God's hands alone.

Agnes and I never forgot our Mother's attitude and advice: "Don't make a serious decision on the spur-of-the-moment; regret is too often a lifetime companion."

Jimmy came to visit Agnes one Saturday night, but she had been called in to work to cover for one of the girls who never reported for her shift. We walked down to the Plaza Theater before her shift ended at eight-thirty to walk her home. The next day, several neighborhood women stopped me to ask who the dapper young man was; so stylishly dressed, as New Yorkers always were. I explained that he was my sister's friend--a band leader from Manhattan. They smiled, remembering his band's performance at the Valentine's Day Dance.

That reminds me of another of my walks into Englewood. I was quite angry about something (though I don't recall what that was) and happened to say: "Dammit!" Well, Patrolman Paddy Murphy came rushing up to me and said, "Young lady, don't let me hear ye use that language again. And, I mean that! Ye don't use language like that around here!" Poor Officer Murphy would surely have a stroke if he heard today's vocabulary!

Everybody liked Paddy Murphy and loved to tell the little story about the time he pulled a car over to question the driver why he hadn't stopped for the traffic light:

"Where are ye from?"

The driver replied: "From Pittsburgh."

"Yeah," Paddy Murphy said, "Well, how come yer license plate says Pennsylvania?" It was all over Englewood; of course, there was no denying his wonderful sense of humor--unless he heard you using "dirty" language.

1942 also brought FDR's Executive Order that authorized the rounding up and relocation of all Japanese people living in the western states. There were some camps in New Jersey which held German and some Italian prisoners of war.

In April, the Office of Price Administration & Civilian Supply (the name later changed to the OPA, the Office of Price Administration), was another governmental agency created by Executive Order to *control inflation*. We all had been conditioned to deprivation during the last decade, but I'd be remiss if I didn't say that there were some who tried to take advantage of the War by raising prices.

Price controls, in some instances, were a good thing, particularly since my sister and I had experienced the greed by those who calculated that with unemployment dropping as it was, the people had more money in their pockets--and the greedy were going to take it.

Agnes and I had gone into Hackensack one afternoon to shop for summer dresses. When we got home and lifted the price sticker that overlaid the regular price tag, we found the dresses had been marked up two dollars. Now, two dollars isn't much by today's standards, but two dollars back then was more like ten dollars in today's economy.

We returned the dresses the next day and told the woman what we had found. You can't imagine the hoops that woman jumped through trying to please us. We took back our money, left the dresses, and told her that we had reported her to the OPA.

Our Mother experienced similar incidents. She did more than her fair share of complaining about lettuce selling for fifteen cents a head, when only the week before it had been ten cents at the store. Can you imagine what my Mother would say if she saw the price of lettuce today?

Ration Books weren't right either!

There was a book for every member in the family, including babies whose books were colored pink; blue books were for children through early teens, and beige books were for mid-teens through adults.

The books authorized *controlled* purchases of food stuffs, such as: meat, butter, sugar, and coffee. Shoes and rubber footwear were purchased with special stamps that also controlled heating oil, gasoline, tires, and larger items, such as: stoves, refrigerators, and the like.

Agnes and I went into Manhattan where we could search the broader selections of things to buy with our ration stamps. Word began circulating that many items would be unavailable--like shoes. Stocks of most everything were dwindling and people soon began standing on lines to buy many an item, only to find that when they reached the counter, the supply had been exhausted. We saw the newsreels showing the British people standing in block-long queues to buy a loaf of bread, or a can of spam. We could only wonder if we were headed for the same fate.

On occasion, a large food store might have a section with certain cuts of beef, above which would be a sign reading: *Today--No Ration Stamps Required.* We always questioned if the so-called "beef" was, in fact, beef--or horse meat, as the rumors circulated.

One memorable recollection about rationing takes me back to a Saturday in late September when Agnes and I went into Manhattan to shop for shoes. I saw a pair that perfectly matched the suit I was wearing. They had "man-made" soles, didn't require a ration coupon, and were only five dollars. What a buy!

The day ended with a beautiful, golden autumn sunset and we thought that a walk across the George Washington Bridge would be more enjoyable than taking a crowded bus back to Englewood. As we walked the pedestrian lane across the wide span of the bridge, I began to feel every inch of the grated walkway, as though I were walking barefooted. By the time we reached the Jersey side, the soles of my shoes were grated layers of pulverized cardboard.

I should have changed my shoes and taken them back to the crook who took my five dollars, but it was getting late and the thought of walking back across the bridge didn't appeal to me. And, need I say that Agnes was nearly in hysterics?

"That's right, Agnes, go ahead and laugh!"

She tried to control her hysteria which only grew louder as she watched me change my shoes.

"It's not at all funny, Agnes! The makers of these shoes used cardboard!" To which she replied: "Well, Margaret, you certainly wouldn't want to be *Walkin' Through Mockin' Bird Lane* in them.

We managed to catch the #86 bus to Palisade Avenue and I had to laugh because Agnes was doing her darndest to control herself, but everyone saw the way her shoulders kept jumping as she tried to stifle her giggles.

While most people seemed to have a little more money in their pockets, it became incredibly difficult locating quality food. Nearly everyone had a "Victory Garden." Our parents had kept a garden for many years in the half acre next to our home. We even had a peach tree at the side of the house beneath our kitchen window. Frozen dinners were introduced and our Mother brought in a few of them, but the taste wasn't to anyone's liking. They did provide the masses of working women with the convenience of not having to wait in lines to buy food--or having to cook after a long day's work.

The clothing manufacturers modified women's dress and suit patterns by decreasing the amount of fabric. However, the decreased fabric didn't lower the price; it went higher. Men's clothing also changed. The People were limited to buying only two pairs of shoes each year, and women's high-heeled shoes were replaced with low heels. Price controls were in place on most everything.

Automobiles ceased to be manufactured, and the People participated in scrap drives, bringing old rubber items, tin, and steel for the few pennies the scrap yards paid. It was customary to refuse payment and donate the proceeds to the war effort.

U.S. Marines landed on Guadalcanal in the Solomon Islands that summer, and we had learned that six of the eight German saboteurs who had been captured for spying were executed, the remaining two were given life sentences as enemy agents.

It gives me pause to think that here we are sixty years later fighting another War--with terrorists entering our Country--and no one is doing very much of anything to stop them at the borders! It can't be ignorance or naive stupidity that has our elected representatives impotent to act--or can it?

Our cousin, Timothy, Packy's brother, died in October after a long and courageous fight with Tuberculosis. Our Mother's older brother, Uncle Jim, sent word that our cousin, John, was on a ship in the Pacific near Guadalcanal. We prayed for him and for all of the boys who had gone off to war, and couldn't help wondering if we'd ever see him again.

We were shopping in Englewood one afternoon when we saw Peter crossing the street with his mother. He was wearing a Navy uniform. It clearly shocked Agnes and I said, "Does this mean that Peter is back in the picture?"

"No. It means you're jumping to conclusions--*again*."

Agnes learned later that he had enlisted after the attack on Pearl Harbor, postponing his high school graduation until after the war, if he survived.

Peter wrote to her, then came calling for a date while on shore leave one weekend. He told us he was stationed at Floyd Bennett Naval Air Field in Far Rockaway, assigned to the son of the man who manufactured *Felsnaphter Soap Products*. (Agnes and Peter were going steady-- *again*.)

In early December, Uncle Jim called to tell Mom that our cousin, John, had gone down on the *USS Juneau*, along with the Sullivan brothers and the entire crew, save a handful of men who had been rescued. The Japanese torpedoed the USS *Juneau* following the Battle of Guadalcanal on a Friday, 13 November 1942.

The holidays approached, bringing with them a deeper sense of foreboding. The war had personally touched our lives with the loss of our cousin. The hometown boy we all knew from the grocery store, who made his Confirmation with Agnes, had enlisted to serve his Country as hundreds of thousands of America's young men were doing immediately following Japan's attack the year before.

Bing Crosby's hit movie, *White Christmas,* came just in time. The song became an instant success, as well it should have. Though its theme of boy-gets-girl had been the standard fare, it reflected the simpler times we all had known as we clung to tender memories of how it used to be.

Jimmy Cagney brought the Country one walloping dose of patriotism with his portrayal of the song-and-dance man, George M. Cohan, in *Yankee Doodle Dandy.* Hollywood even cast an actor to play Roosevelt, who needed all the good PR he could get. Ironically, and sadly, the popular Vaudevillian, George M. Cohan, died that November.

1943

Our politicians made America's employers their official tax collectors of the Peoples' money. I guess they all took comfort in the fact that *As Time Goes By* the mounting Federal Debt of $142.7-Billion would eventually be paid. Federal Spending, as reported, had climbed to $78.56-Billion. The politicians must have been jubilant, singing the popular war song, "*They're Either Too Young, or Too Old... They're either too gray or too grassy green. The pickings are poor and the crop is lean. What's good is in the Army, what's left will never harm me...*"

Lucky for Roosevelt, unemployment dropped to its lowest, only 1.9% and the populace shifted their anger to the *Japs* and *Krauts* who were killing our boys.

I was on my way to being twenty-one in the Fall; Agnes had just turned nineteen and was spending hours at the kitchen table with her cups of tea writing to former classmates and to all the boys she had dated.

Agnes and I stepped outside one afternoon, the snow gently falling around us as we stood on that narrow path. Agnes was filled with sorrow for so many of the young men whose letters carried thoughts of home and loved ones.

"They never question why they're there," she said; I could see tears in her eyes.

"They talk of coming home and doing things they had never

given any thought to before," she said. "And, so many of them will never be coming home."

"That's war, Agnes," I said, without knowing how to comfort her. "Roosevelt, Hitler, Churchill, Stalin, Mussolini, and that Jap Hirohito should face each other and fight! It's their war!"

The snow fell, covering the narrow path where we stood. "I'll print that on a little tag and hang it on a *String of Pearls* for everybody to see," she said, tilting her hand, palm-up, to catch the snowflakes.

The war letters continued to come from all over the world. I'd see Agnes frowning as she read her V-mail letters that had whole sections blackened by military censors whose job it was to maintain secrecy. I answered my letters, too, though I was still dating Sam. Agnes, on the other hand, had not committed to any of the young men she had dated.

In the meantime, Frank Sinatra was causing major traffic jams. Streets in and around Times Square were overflowing with hysterical teenaged girls waiting in lines to purchase tickets for his performances at the Paramount. The skinny young crooner from Hoboken, New Jersey, had become the heartthrob of millions of young ladies, their mothers included!

Roosevelt traveled to Morocco to meet Winston Churchill for the Casablanca Conference that January. Agnes joked that he must have seen Humphrey Bogart's *Casablanca* and thought he might find Ingrid Bergman waiting there. "She didn't wait for Bogie, she sure wouldn't wait for FDR," Agnes said.

The government imposed an "entertainment tax" on everything they deemed "unnecessary," such as theater tickets, cigarettes, nightclubs, and the like. The income tax withholding scheme had done what it was intended to do--guarantee quarterly deposits into the U.S. Treasury.

News came from most everyone we knew: our cousin, Packy, was in the Army Engineering Corps, and Jimmy Cummings was training to be a medical technician with the Army at Camp Pickett in Blackstone, Virginia.

In early February, Agnes and I thought we might consider working at Bendix Aviation Corporation and took the bus out to their employment office in Teterboro, New Jersey. We heard their wages were the highest; in fact, they were higher than those paid to men *before* the War!

We filled out the employment applications and waited our turn to be interviewed. The manager called us both into his office. He sat down at his desk, lifted our applications, gave us the "once over" then said, "You young ladies would not be suited to this work."

Though we left a little disappointed, he was right. We always wore dresses or skirted suits, stockings, heeled shoes, gloves and hats; dressing in overhauls and boots and pushing heavy equipment didn't seem like reality.

Reality was for the men who felt *Somebody Else is Taking My Place* after they'd gone off to war. It was good that there were so many women willing and able to do the work that men had previously done but, of course, they were being paid more money than the men had been paid. For the majority of those women, their entry into the workplace had instilled a sense of competitiveness which the men, upon their return, regarded as lost femininity.

I cannot ignore my own sense of independence; to do so would be hypocritical. Using patriotism and the home front War effort seemed ripe for "the end justifying the means" mentality. I saw a small part of the female population rearranging their priorities, as though they had been "conditioned." (Needless to say, the *baby boom* never would have occurred if that "conditioning" had taken complete hold. I dare say, most of the women who had that taste of independence and having made more money than had the men prior to the war, must have left some indelible impressions. Otherwise, how did we get so many *femiNazis,* as Rush Limbaugh calls them?)

With all the billions of dollars spent *prior* to the War, the People asked: *why* did we spend so many billions of dollars and expend so much effort making war materiel that we gave away under Lend Lease? In hindsight, it seems that economics and some grand plan for the restructuring of society had to have played some part--not just for the years immediately following the War, but far into the future.

The casualty numbers of American dead continued, even from within our little hometown. *The Bergen Evening Record* published the names of the men who had been killed in battle after battle, as more and more gold-trimmed flags hung in windows proudly, but sadly, announcing to passersby that a loved one had paid the supreme sacrifice. It was nearly impossible to hold back the tears as we walked to Englewood or Hackensack.

We were a nation at war; a nation constrained by price controls and little to buy. We were a nation at war without war protesters, entertainers sympathetic to our enemies, or a media hellbent on undermining the Commander-in-Chief and the generals who waged a war the People never wanted. But then, the People of my generation were patriotic, respecting the sacrifices our young men and women were making. We may not have liked that our leaders had taken us to war, but we respected America's stand against despotism and evil.

Our parents had given us a generous sum of money at Christmas because, as Mom had said, "Yer grown-up now and ye can better buy for yer'selves than we can. Besides, ye'll be smart to go into Manhattan with yer ration books and buy a few things before there's nothing left to buy!" Agnes and I talked about a shopping trip into the City, but she felt we could put the money to better use.

"What better use?" I asked her.

"Well, you know how Stella always talked about the South..." she said, then continued without giving me a chance to respond. "And Martin Block did say that 'you'll never see through the eyes of forty what you can see through the eyes of twenty... You're already twenty-one, Margaret! We should see the South, or you'll be too old to appreciate it!"

Agnes was quite serious. The look in her eyes confirmed it, as did the firm position of her lips when she made up her mind. "Exactly *where* in the South did you have in mind?" I thought about our little cache in that decorated tin.

"We could go to Atlanta."

"We don't have enough money to go to Atlanta," I said. "Besides, Rhett Butler won't be there."

She rolled her eyes. "What about Virginia?"

"Why Virginia?" I suspected why.

"We could see Richmond or Williamsburg...or Norfolk."

"And which boyfriend is stationed in Norfolk?" I asked.

"I don't have a boyfriend in Norfolk or Richmond," she said rather indignantly.

"Peter isn't in Norfolk?"

Her eyebrow arched. "No. He's in Portland, Maine when he's not on that mine sweeper! The others are at boot camps, on ships, or in Italy or England."

Her boyfriends may have written that she should *Do Nothin' Til You Hear from Me...* but, their *nothin'* and her *nothin'* were two different things. The sailors, soldiers, Marines, and Air Force fly-boys all wanted to date and become engaged to Agnes. But, Agnes wasn't ready to settle down. Art was her first love, the movies her second, and Peter, Bill, or Jimmy a "maybe" third, as best I could tell. But, to get back to our "trip." We told our Mother that we were going to take a trip to Virginia.

"Oh, no, yer not!"

"I'm twenty-one," I said.

"And I'm yer Mother and yer not takin' a trip to Virginia or anywhere else!"

In truth, our parents knew that I was the closest thing to an Army Staff Sergeant who knew how to tell the boys to "*Straighten up and Fly Right"* left, or out of the way entirely. (Which I always did, knowing that the young men were on leave or, perhaps, being shipped out, and wanted to court a pretty girl.)

After our brief conversation with Mom, we thought we'd bring up the subject again at supper with Dad there to voice his opinions. We were positive and happy about the possibility.

Dad was very good about listening and was fair in the decisions he made; either listening to us and supporting our position, or agreeing with our Mother and reinforcing her preference about a matter. After supper, we ventured into the idea.

"Yer not going. I've heard all I'm going to about it. It's not what young ladies do; traveling alone in these times, with a war going on and servicemen going back and forth from one state to another. No, my word's final and don't bring it up again."

Dad intervened: "Well, you might want to talk with Evelyn, or her mother," Dad said. "She's back, you know. She made a trip to see her husband."

(Evelyn and her mother were neighbors living a block away. And, yes, Evelyn did tell us that he was in service and always shared the news of how he was doing.)

"I'm sure she didn't have any problems or, certainly, somebody would have heard about it by now," Dad said.

"We're talking about two different people," Mom said, placing her tea cup on the saucer. "She's older than the girls. She's a married woman. She was going to see her *husband*..." Mom went on about all the reasons why we couldn't go.

"Why don't you take a walk up there," Dad said. "Talk with Evelyn and her mother and see how they look at things. You know, everything changes during wartime. The conveniences that were available in peacetime no longer exist. Let's wait and see what Evelyn and her mother have to say," Dad said, looking at Mom. "If it sounds like a risk then, no, the girls shouldn't go. They'll have to accept your word on the matter and stay home."

Not another word was spoken about it over the course of the evening, however, the next day after supper, it seemed as if Mom's resistance to our idea had diminished. We suspected that Mom and Dad had a private conversation about the matter the night before.

I ventured into the discussion again, "We should find out how much the train tickets will be... if we can go directly to Richmond, or to Williamsburg."

"Wait a minute!" Dad said. "You can't just get a train reservation--not in a few days. The military men have priority. In fact, whole trains are commandeered for the troops moving them from one base to another, or to naval yards to ship out."

"Then, how are we going to get there?" I asked, disappointed that we couldn't go by train because they'd been represented so well in the motion pictures we had seen.

"You know, people do travel by bus," Agnes said. "There's nothing wrong with a bus."

"Like the bus we take to Hackensack?" I asked.

"No. There are more comfortable buses, designed for traveling a distance," she said. "Why don't you go get a brochure from the Greyhound station and you'll see." That was something I had just learned. "I didn't know that." (In my usual pattern of going about my own business, I hadn't *kept up* with the progress around me.)

Dad returned to the table with a cup of coffee. "I thought I mentioned it--that's the way Evelyn went. She said it wasn't bad at all. The passengers she met were mostly mothers and wives going to see sons and husbands in camp. They were traveling from all over the country," he said, spooning some sugar into his cup.

"I'll make the telephone call," Agnes said. "I'll find out the prices and availability of tickets."

The next day, Agnes made her call. That night after supper, she brought pages of notes to the table and we talked it all over with our Dad, and the following cold February day, the tickets were purchased for our short four-day trip to Virginia.

The temperatures dipped into the teens and it was freezing and snowing. To our surprise, we learned that the *sun doesn't always shine in Dixie*. But, we did see Washington, D.C., our nation's capitol, and traveled on to Richmond where we toured the Museum, had dinner and checked into a hotel. Early the next morning, we boarded the Greyhound bus to Williamsburg to see one of the first settlements in the Country.

We did meet a number of wives and mothers who were traveling to Norfolk to see their husbands and sons before they shipped out. It wasn't on our itinerary, but we were curious and did get to see Norfolk, too. The little seaport town overflowed with sailors, its docks off-limits to all civilians so, we never did get to see any of the ships in port.

Our four-hour stay in Norfolk allowed us time only for lunch and a movie. We saw *Casablanca* (again) then, boarded the bus for Richmond, and home. We two young ladies felt so grown-up, traveling far from home to places we had never seen before. (And, freezing every bit of the way!)

Sam found out about our "trip" and, eventually, got over the fact that we had traveled so far from home during wartime. He was accustomed to meeting me either before, or just after, I left work, and we'd go into Manhattan. Sometimes he'd take me to dinner in Chinatown or we'd go to Battery Park and then catch a movie. He had a frosty sense of humor that camouflaged his disappointment over not being able to join the Marines. They had immediately detected a heart murmur which precluded him from being accepted.

I continued working and Agnes went on with her art classes and ushering at the Plaza Theater. Gone were those happy and playful days when cousin Packy and Jimmy came to visit and enjoy the country beauty of Englewood, sixty-three years ago.

The war letters kept coming and Agnes continued to answer and write the young men she had known--until a long silence ensued, and then learned the boy had been a casualty of the war. Working at the Plaza couldn't have been easy for her, seeing repeat performances of *The Fleet's In, Navy Blues,* and *Kiss the Boys Goodbye*.

Patriotism ran thick in her blood; she honored and prayed for those who served, said the Pledge of Allegiance at gatherings, and sang our National Anthem on Memorial Day, along with hundreds of others who went to town to remember, promising never to forget.

Peter was on a mine sweeper somewhere in the Atlantic, and Jimmy was about to be shipped out of the Country to only God knew where.

Jimmy wrote Agnes from Camp Pickett and invited her (along with yours truly, of course) to visit him in July. Our Mother didn't object to this trip. He wrote that his mother had prepared a package for us to bring to him in Virginia. And so, we went into Manhattan to visit his mother and pick-up the small box she had packed for her son.

Our Mother bought us each a new piece of luggage, and Dad added to our rip money by folding a ten-dollar bill into our hands saying: "In case you see something you'd like to buy..." as they said their goodbyes at the Greyhound bus station.

The trip to Virginia in February had been tolerable, even in the dead of winter but, July was a sweltering month to be heading South. The tree-lined boulevards filled with historic sites through Washington, D.C., and the crossing over the Potomac River into Virginia was one of the most picturesque sights we'd seen. The drive through Richmond, the Confederacy's capitol during the Civil War, onto historic Petersburg, and then Southwest to Blackstone and Camp Pickett gave us another representation of the South below the Mason-Dixon Line.

We learned that the Camp had been established some time in the 1880s and was officially dedicated the previous year on July 3rd, marking the 79th Anniversary of General George S. Pickett's historic charge at Gettysburg, in Pennsylvania. Most of the huge military base was off-limits to civilians; there was no doubting the significance of the Camp with its airfield, rows-upon-rows of barracks that housed the enlisted men, chapels, theaters, several NCO and Officer's Clubs, the post office, and a hospital where Jimmy worked as a medical technician.

We, along with other visiting women, were housed in a barracks in the visitors' area, which Agnes and I thought profoundly inconvenient. It was swell for men but, in our opinion, not nearly adequate for women. Of course, the thinking could have been to impress upon wives, sisters, mothers, and girlfriends, that as "rough" as living was in a post barracks, some foxhole on a battlefield had to be worse, if not totally inconceivable.

Jimmy took us to the amphitheater to see the 1940 film, *Rhythm On the River* with Bing Crosby and Mary Martin. It was a delightful musical and so very appropriate because Bing Crosby's role was as a composer, and Mary Martin's a lyricist--both of whom personified Jimmy's pre-enlistment years when he wrote his own music and lyrics.

On Saturday evening, Jimmy invited us to join him at the Officer's Club where he had been playing piano for the officers and their visiting wives and families. I remained seated at our table while

Jimmy led Agnes to the bench at the piano. Half way into his opening song, officers and their companions encircled the piano four deep. No matter where Sergeant Cummings was--if a piano was close by--so, too, would one find Jimmy, his fingers flying over the ivory keys as he played the most beautiful music of our time.

Having known the young Irishman for three years, our three-day visit at Camp Pickett represented the depth of our friendship for our cousin's best friend who had become ours as well.

Jimmy saw us off at the bus, sending his best wishes to our parents, and hugs and kisses to his Mother and sister. Within a few months, Agnes received a letter from him. He was "shipping out" with his medical unit.

The following month, General George Patton landed in Sicily, ahead of England's Montgomery. General Douglas MacArthur took a strategic island in New Guinea, and in September, we learned that Jimmy sailed for England aboard the HMS Mauritania.

Peter was ever constant throughout Agnes' life, from the time she was a little girl of twelve. He and Jimmy had met a few times when Peter had shore leave and walked Agnes home from the theater. The two were rivals, though Agnes hadn't quite made up her mind about either one of them. At nineteen, with more than enough dates, and boys off at War, becoming "serious" was the furthest thing from her mind.

No matter where we went, young men took note; as one day in Manhattan. The 5th Avenue bus came to a stop and as I got off the bus, six young men in uniform rushed to help Agnes down the steps of the bus. I--quickly and forcefully--pushed my way through the ring of soldiers to the door. "Make way for the lady!" One would have thought she was a celebrity with all of the attention being shown her. She blushed and quietly stepped down with a shy smile of appreciation. That did it!

"You have to stop doing that, Agnes! It only encourages them," I said, as we walked further down the street.

"I know."

"Then, why do you do it?"

"Because a smile is a harmless show of appreciation."

"Right! And I'm left to fend them off. How ungrateful! At this rate, I might as well be in a uniform which would certainly discourage them!"

She stopped short and I nearly ran into her. "Don't you dare do such a thing!"

That settled it; she did appreciate me after all.

Clouds of uncertainty hung heavy in those months as increasing reports of the War filled the newspapers and theater newsreels. Going to the movies was a two-fold experience; we saw the black-and-white reality of war--as approved by the War Department--of our brave young men fighting thousands of miles away in Italy, or in the South Pacific, sinking Japanese ships, or fighting in dense island jungles which civilization appeared to have overlooked.

Just before Thanksgiving, Britain's Air Force bombed Berlin and Roosevelt traveled to Cairo, Egypt, to meet Winston Churchill and Chiang Kai-Shek, the leader of the Republic of China to discuss the defeat of Japan. A week later, FDR and Churchill were in Tehran, Iran, to meet "Uncle Joe" Stalin. History later reported, it's where the three devised *Operation Overlord,* the Allies' plan to invade Europe to destroy Hitler and his Third Reich.

The Country's Christmas present was Roosevelt's announcement that Dwight D. Eisenhower would be the *Supreme Allied Commander,* and the Mills Brothers sang *Paper Doll.*

Tears ran heavy through the holidays as loved ones' letters carried the hopes of the song, *I'll Be Home For Christmas*, while most prayed "if only it were so."

Before Charlie left for England, he called to ask if he could visit me. "I want us to become engaged." I had already postponed any engagement in February and this would be the second. With a few words spoken for a commitment of a lifetime, or for that moment's peace of mind, or sense of emotional security, I could not accept his offer of marriage as anything but a very foolish mistake.

It was not unusual for young men going off to war to advance the idea of marriage. He wanted a special someone waiting for his return. While everyone was certainly praying that he would return, it was a terrible "unknown."

I knew many young people who made the mistake of rushing into marriage and regretted it afterwards. For some, their young man never came home yet, in their minds, he was the "only perfect one" who came into her life. Who could say whether it was true or not?

I suppose it's part of the heartbreak of war; when two young people are caught up in that unknown glimpse of destiny, with not nearly enough time for an understanding of the other. And if the young man never returned, the girl might spend the rest of her life lost in the heartbreak of having loved the boy whose promise was fated never to be fulfilled.

While Agnes and I were like other girls, we were not inclined to youth's hopeless romanticism. We were grounded in reality; believed that friendship was held, while commitment was reserved.

Our Mother's guiding temperament prevailed: "No matter what life brings yer way, yer dignity can never be taken. What ye value highly, ye'll not give away cheaply."

1944

Federal Spending reportedly reached $91.30-Billion; with a National Debt of $204.1-Billion, with unemployment scarcely recordable at 1.2%.

FDR decided to *Ac-Cent-Tchu-Ate the Positive* and canceled his Works Progress Administration. Why he waited so long was a mystery to most people because our men had traded their picks and hammers for rifles, uniforms, and boots to slop through mud fighting in Southern Europe, in Japanese-held jungles, or buried at sea along with millions of tons of steel that *Rosie the Riveter* had welded together.

The Japanese bombed us at Pearl Harbor but, Roosevelt had put an embargo around the Japanese Island which many considered an act of war. And after we were at war, somehow, it didn't seem to matter that Japan remained Russia's *ally*--while Russia was *our* ally and FDR was sending them millions of dollars in war materiel under his Lend Lease program. (Does anyone know if Russia ever repaid us?)

How Little We Know of the dirty, behind-the-scenes machinations of those who rule the masses. *I'm Beginning to See the Light* had a special meaning for many of us during those War years. I suppose for some of our WWII veterans the criticism goes even deeper--and justly so.

Our troops were still battling the Germans for control of Italy; while our ships and submarines were attacking Japanese fleets, and countless thousands of our men were invading the Japanese-held strongholds in the Pacific.

Peter was transferred to the USS Firm, the flag ship of the

commander of the mine sweeper's division 24, at Casco Bay in Portland, Maine. While on leave one day in late January, he came for a date with Agnes. When they returned, she showed us the engagement ring Peter had brought her, and said they would be getting married in August with a military wedding in Portland. *Don't Fence Me In* was the tune that popped into my head.

Agnes loved to flirt and write to the boys *Over There* so, I never really thought she would decide to marry so soon. But, that was Agnes--unpredictable, always having a mind of her own, and never providing an explanation for the decisions she made. Besides, she could always change her mind. She always joked about her fickle ways: "What I liked yesterday, I may not like today...and, what I like today, I may hate tomorrow!" Need I say more?

Agnes, of course, would continue to live at home until the war ended, but all that was still months away. Couples who had married before or during the war usually lived with the girl's parents because rented rooms and apartment accommodations were at a premium. Few could find housing no matter how much they paid though all rents were controlled by the OPA. House after house was being converted into two-family dwellings which still didn't answer the demand.

In February, we learned that American planes were bombing sites throughout Germany. Everyone prayed that the War would soon come to an end.

In early Spring, just about everything became harder to get and incredibly scarce. We stood on lines waiting to buy sugar and just about everything else. And, nylons were impossible to find.

Agnes had the morning phone shift at the Plaza and met me at the decorating shop. We walked to Whalens Soda Fountain, looked over the menu, then ordered two egg salad sandwiches. (We didn't eat meat on Friday.)

The waitress said there wasn't any egg salad. We asked for a grilled cheese sandwich. There wasn't any cheese either. In fact, there wasn't anything for sandwiches--not even the bread. We then asked for two cups of tea and a scoop of vanilla ice cream on a piece of pound cake that we would share. "Sorry, no ice cream and no pound cake either!" I believe we had a few soda crackers and our cup of hot tea.

We all prayed a little deeper, wished a little harder, and did without more than just a little. There didn't seem to be any balance in life. People were working and earning considerably more money than they had prior to the war, but anything that became available (though controlled by the OPA) was much higher priced than before. Those hardships certainly taught my generation to save for the unexpected. How often I've heard throughout my life, how *thrifty... stingy*, even *cheap* my generation is. Today's young people would had to have walked in our shoes to appreciate why we are the way we are.

The parallel I see now, is that while our current President has passed tax cuts, and the Government Accounting Office reports "no inflation and lower unemployment statistics," many of the people I know are in serious debt. They try to pay the inflated prices of houses and the ever-escalating price of gasoline that has driven up the cost of food, clothing, and everything else we need to survive. I believe that it could only be to the Peoples' advantage if our so-called "representatives" implemented price controls which would be one way of protecting the Peoples' money.

It's a Sentimental Journey in this mind of mine as I recall so many long ago days. I have to laugh as I think of one very pretty afternoon in May...

My boss was going into the City and gave me the afternoon off that day and, so, I decided to take a bus to Newark. I was walking down one of the busy city streets and passed a recruiting office. One would have to be blind not to see the huge poster that promoted the WAACs. Yes, you guessed it! This war-hating fusspot actually went into the recruiting office. I think I was being "nosy" rather than patriotic. I didn't really approve of women in service, but I felt I needed to know what it was all about. If one never asks, one never knows, I always believed.

I completed the application form, let them check my weight, blood pressure, and heart rhythm. Then, the recruiting officer brought me in for an interview and explained that there would be long hours doing clerical work, inventorying uniforms, and the like. He gave me a list of job classifications and said he would wait for the results of the preliminary "physical." I thought how much can they tell from taking only a blood pressure reading and listening to my heartbeat.

It felt like a repeat of the day we had gone to Bendix Aviation. I knew deep down that I really didn't have any intention of joining the WAACs, or any other branch of service that had opened up to women. And, after a walk through busy downtown Newark, I boarded the bus for home, and thought: *what a crazy thing to do!* I saw the routine and responsibilities of my life changing in such a dramatic way that I was momentarily caught up in a sudden urge to escape. I smiled. My only escape was back to Teaneck Road for the walk home; the visit with the WAACS had consumed the afternoon, leaving no time to shop.

When I arrived home, later than my usual arrival time, Agnes was setting the table for supper and said, "Where were you?" I explained that I had gone into Newark.

"I wish I had the afternoon off, I could have had the chance to shop, too," she said. "Why did you just go off like that?"

"My boss gave me the afternoon off and I wanted to do something different," I said. "I enjoyed it very much."

"What did you buy?"

Now, at this point, I knew I couldn't admit what I had *really* done while in Newark. My stopping at the WAACS wasn't sensible and not important enough to mention because I knew nothing was going to come of it.

"Sam called and is on his way over," Agnes said.

Sam was very vocal about what he thought and he made me laugh, both of which I liked. He came from a family of three sisters and one brother. His mother had died when he was a little boy and was raised by his older sisters and his father who was a master machinist. His father also owned a small clock shop on Main Street in Hackensack where he also repaired antique clocks and guns. There wasn't anything he couldn't design or fix and Sam followed in his footsteps, helping to repair clocks and guns, as well as being an experienced locksmith while holding a full-time job at a chemical plant in East Rutherford.

Sam came by, had supper with us, and we all had a pleasant time. We all talked about the War, which annoyed Sam because his brother was oversees and he wasn't. We listened to a few radio shows and called it an evening, morning came all too quickly.

The War dragged on and the songs reflected the pain of separation. Harry James' hit that year was *I'll Get By...* Bing Crosby sang his heart out with *I Love You ...* Frank Sinatra sang *I Fall in Love Too Easily* and, nearly all the young women wrote their sailors and soldiers... *You Belong to My Heart.* It was one of Sam's favorites.

Agnes' letter writing came to an end months before, otherwise Peter's jealous streak never would have been quelled.

In June, Dino (another fellow I had been dating) gave me an engagement ring. We had gone out a few times over the course of eight or ten months so, it came as quite a surprise. To tell the truth, young men back then were no different than the fellows who went off to fight in Korea, VietNam, or in Iraq. I liked Dino, but not enough to marry him. It wasn't right for me to take his ring; and I didn't.

Then, it was June 6. Everyone was caught up in the news bulletins: the Allied forces landed on the beaches in France, across the English Channel, at Normandy. It was D-Day!

The radio announcer said it was the largest assault ever mounted in the history of warfare with thousands of airplanes and ships and over a hundred-thousand soldiers and sailors. The invasion of Europe came at a high cost to the United States; which killed thousands and maimed thousands more.

Sam came calling that evening and we walked down to Englewood, remembering only days earlier our walk into town for the Memorial Day observance and prayers for our armed forces. I remember how he nonchalantly put his arm around my waist, guiding me through the passersby. I also remember Paddy Murphy's thick Irish brogue: "Get yer hands off of that young lady and don't let me catch ye hanging on to her again!" Sam held his temper, rather than create a scene, and explained that he was being a gentleman, navigating me through the crush of people on the sidewalk.

In Paddy Murphy's eyes (and most everyone else's), a young

man's arm around a girl's waist was considered a sign of disrespect. This may be difficult for some to understand, but my generation has been in culture shock for nearly fifty years. The slow, but deliberate deterioration of our society's morals has left most of us thinking we dropped out of a time-warp.

The heat of July was soon upon us as we rushed about in a whirlwind of preparations for Agnes' wedding day. Peter announced that his Mother was not able to make the trip to Maine for their military wedding; so, to accommodate her, they made arrangements for the wedding at St. Cecelia's Church. The short notice curtailed their wedding plans--not that they had planned an elaborate wedding-- and chose a simple Nuptial Mass that would be said on Monday, August 14. Few people in those days had money enough to spend on lavish weddings and, even if our parents had the money, we were too conservative to allow the sacrament of holy matrimony to be upstaged by the trapping of pretentiousness.

The week before their wedding, Agnes and I went to Patterson, the city where the Colt-Patterson gun had been manufactured. We were going to Mayer Brothers Department Store, a beautiful and elegant establishment that had opened in the 1880s. I recall the majestic staircase in the center of the store and that our purchases went far beyond what we had planned to buy. Agnes bought a few dresses and some linens, and the few things she would need for her honeymoon trip.

Our parents' wedding gift was a Waterfall styled bedroom suite that went into the bedroom she and I had shared. I moved into the bedroom at the rear of the house.

The famous Palisades Amusement Park, which families from both sides of the Hudson River frequented since the late 1880s burned the week before their wedding. It reopened the following year, in time for the returning servicemen who had spent many a day when they were little boys. We, too, had gone there as little girls and loved the cotton candy. In later years, our dates always tried to get us to join them on the *daring* rides; and try as they did, they settled for the *tamer* spins and whirls.

I remember the night before the wedding and seeing Agnes packing her suitcase for their honeymoon trip to the Pennsylvania mountains. Neither of us got much sleep, and Agnes often reminded me how I sat on the corner of her bed and asked, "Are you sure you want to go through with this?"

She just looked at me, laughed, and said: "What do you want to do, Margaret...catch a bus and go South?"

Of course, I was happy for her that she was going to marry Peter, who had always been a gentleman. No one could dispute that he always had shown a particular interest in her since he was that skinny boy working at the grocery store in Englewood in 1936.

Their wedding day arrived--sunny and hot. We had tea together and Dad called for a taxi to drive us to the Church. He walked Agnes down the aisle as the pipe organ in the loft played the *Ave Maria*. She wore a beautiful but conservative dress, a dainty little white hat, high-heeled white shoes, and gloves.

Peter stood at the altar railing in his Navy blues and that familiar broad smile that said he'd won the heart of the girl he set out to capture. His brother was his best man and I, my sister's maid of honor. Pastor Anslam Werner said Mass and performed the ceremony.

Afterwards, everyone came to our home for lunch; we snapped a few pictures of Agnes and Peter standing on the pathway beside the house, then everyone kissed them goodbye and they left to catch the bus to Hackensack for a Greyhound that would take them to Pennsylvania for their week-long honeymoon. (There was no car at their disposal because there was no gasoline to fill it.)

Sam came to see me each afternoon while Agnes and Peter were away. He was delighted to have attended their wedding and I had the sense that his intentions were growing more serious. (One life-altering event was all I could handle at the time!) He was my friend *first* and though quite comical, his serious side was that of a very matured and dependable young man. *But*, I still wasn't ready for marriage.

The afternoon my sister and new brother-in-law returned, Agnes walked Peter to the bus stop for his trip back to Portland and one of the mine sweepers that would be sent out to patrol for German U-boats and ships.

The Allies were liberating one country after another in their continuing onslaught against Hitler's divisions. Paris was freed at the end of August. Brussels in September. In October, *The Adventures of Ozzie and Harriet* came to us, though I didn't particularly care for it.

Out of one of those little recesses in my mind, I see the beautiful "tuxedo" coat that Agnes bought that October. It was an unusual shade of dark gray with a jet black velvet border sewn to both front panels that ran all the way around the stand-up collar. She bought it at Gimbels in Manhattan where we always managed to find really unusual selections.

Heads turned every time she wore that coat. Some of her girlfriends asked her to sew black velvet panels on their coats. Agnes obliged, but to tell the truth, as good as her sewing was, not one of their coats came close to looking as stylish as the one Agnes wore.

"You either got it or you don't," Connie said. "And, Aggie, you got it!"

Agnes blushed and shook her head.

"And, Pete's a darn lucky guy," Connie added, though a little disappointed that her own handsome brother hadn't sufficiently impressed Agnes. "I thought you might wind-up as my sister," she said, then slapped a hand on my back: "And you, too, Margie!" That was Connie, a friend and comical pal who buddied around with us whenever she caught up with doing her father's bookkeeping.

It was also a chilly Sunday in late October when Agnes and I waited in the line that wrapped around the block at the Paramount

Theater to see Frank Sinatra. The crowd of waiting young girls were known as "bobby-soxers" and you can be sure that Agnes and I did not wear bobby sox. We wore nylon stockings and high-heeled shoes.

One notable distinction in wearing stockings is that it was not unusual for a young lady to excuse herself to go to the *Powder Room* where she would straighten the seams of her stockings(!) Being "off-center" was simply not acceptable. Another strict mode of fashion was to wear gloves and a hat. Hats were very popular and a hat could create the "finished" look of a young lady's whole attire. Hats were quite costly but despite a young lady's limited budget for a wardrobe, a hat was indispensable. Agnes and I were no different. Today, however, hats are as obsolete as some articles of clothing, such as bras and, sometimes, even panties. Hankies were always carried by ladies back then, too. (Those of us who remember ladies' hankies will admit that our hankies were bigger than what women wear as panties today.)

That October was as beautiful as all the others I remember. A glorious array of trees in every shade and color adorned the streets as chestnut-laden branches hung over sidewalks beneath bright blue, cloudless skies as the bite of winter's approach trailed in the crisp clean air.

Halloween came, and so, too, the little goblins, galloping cowboys, and tippy-toe ballerinas all with funny paper masks, and their brown bags filled with Halloween goodies from trick-or-treating.

October's masqueraders retreated, allowing yet another procession of masked faces for Election Day. Roosevelt won an unprecedented *fourth* term, defeating Thomas E. Dewey. Many in the Country objected to Roosevelt, however, I do believe that fear kept the majority of the People from making a change because we were so deeply engaged in war. He had three terms--twelve years--to fulfill his promises; and in the end, The *Great* Depression was conquered only by a world going to War.

Sam called early that Election Day morning. "We have a few hours off, but I've already told my boss that I need the whole day off...and I want you to do the same. We're going into New York. Take care of your voting, and I'll be by to pick you up before lunch." The invitation was most appealing: standing on line to cast my ballot and then returning to work? The idea of spending the rest of that beautiful day with Sam in Manhattan posed not one moment's hesitation as to which course I would choose.

Lower Manhattan was our favorite haunt. We walked to Battery Park, across from Ellis Island, where we strolled among the population of Lower Manhattan that was Italian, Asian, and Jewish. One vivid memory from that date with Sam is walking down a street filled with vendors hawking their wares. One man stood beside his fold-up stool on which was his suitcase of products. Suddenly, he swept up his suitcase in one hand and snatched the little stool with the other, then raced down the street as a New York City policeman crossed the thoroughfare. It wasn't hard to understand why; street vendors had to have a vendor's license and when they didn't, their actions confirmed the fact.

Agnes and I had an experience with one such vendor when we each bought a pair of nylons. When we got home, we opened the package to find that both pairs were shredded with runs.

It was a day long trip that allowed Sam and I to enjoy the look of old Manhattan that was so different then to the way the City looks today. We arrived home close to ten o'clock in the evening. Agnes, Mom and Dad were having tea and listening to the commentator's reporting of the election results.

Agnes had her own news to convey. Before Sam brought me home, Agnes had told our parents that a baby was due in late Spring. I thought: *Oh, my. This is going to be a new experience!* I was surprised and delighted to hear the news. It was the natural wish of every married couple and, particularly, during a time of war when fate was the master of everyone's destiny. My next thought was that we won't be going into Manhattan to shop for make-up or clothes--it would be baby "things," which I knew nothing about.

I had been working long hours at the decorating shop and along about mid-November, I had a second job at the Englewood Theater. It was a smaller theater than the Plaza and they needed a cashier. I thought that would be perfect; I could leave my full-time job, have a bite of supper, and go on to the theater for a few hours.

The manager was a middle-aged widow lady who had been a teacher. I was there about three weeks, when one evening as I was closing out and preparing the cash report of the ticket sales, my manager came to me and asked if I would like to work for her full time. I explained that I already had a full-time job, a bit confused that she hadn't remembered my noting that on my resume.

She said: "I'm offering you the position of assistant manager with a salary of forty-two dollars a week." I thought: *how could I? I've never been in management; what do I know about managing a theater?*

After an hour-long conversation, during which my manager explained the responsibilities of the position, she said: "I'd like you to trust it enough to give it a try. I believe you would be very good as my assistant." Naturally, I told her I would have to give my other boss notice, which she respected.

I left with a feeling of importance.

The next afternoon, I told everyone about the new job that was offered to me. The four of us sat sipping our tea at the kitchen table after supper before I left for the theater for my part-time job. Mom said, "That's not really a job for a young woman. Management is a man's job."

Dad was very supportive of the opportunity presented to me. "If

I was young again, I would be involved in some way with the entertainment industry--even if it was the business side of it. I like the feeling of people going places for a pleasurable time, especially to escape life's everyday troubles and demands," he said. "That was how I viewed the theatrical jobs I was fortunate to have had so long ago," he added, pouring another cup of coffee. "I think you should accept the position, Margaret. If you don't like it, there are certainly other jobs around."

Agnes had her views, too. "Now *you'll* be paid to go into the City for the lobby cards," she said. "If it was me, I'd take it. Besides, look at all the movies you'll get to see!"

"You wouldn't be seeing the movies, you'd be sitting in an office," I said.

"Well, that might make a difference," she said, laughing. "But, you will know which movies are coming before anyone else." Agnes had that happy spirit and no matter what the drawback, there was the good side to discover. For Agnes, the cup was always half full; for me, it was approaching empty.

War nearly broke out on Manhattan Avenue one late November evening after two officers from the WAAC's Army recruiting office came to my home to see me. And, how lucky I was to be at work. Had I any foresight of what I was coming home to, I'd have left town.

Mom and Agnes were furious that I had "secretly gone to enlist!" My Mother told the recruiters: "My daughter is not going into the WAACs and I don't want any encouragement from anyone--do ye understand?"

There was no way I could explain--but, I tried...

In chorus, Mom and Agnes said: "What kind of thing was that to do?" It wasn't a question; it was a demand to know.

"If we couldn't get hired at Bendix because we didn't fit the mold, Margaret, how did you think you'd fit in the WAACs?" Agnes asked through her own incredulity.

I explained that it had been nothing more than a curiosity, but neither of them would listen to a word I said. Dad had been noncommittal during their three-day excursion into disbelief. I certainly didn't tell Sam about the event; I'd have remembered because he was every bit as outspoken as my mother and sister. So, outside of my parents and sister, you folks are the only ones who know that I did such an unthinkable thing! I must admit that I really did feel stupid, especially since I was so completely against women in the Army in the first place.

Maybe doing the absurd was all I could think to do. My sister's marriage had changed our routine--even though, in the past, we had separate work schedules and dates with our boyfriends.

Martin Block was so right... "you *can't see through the eyes of a forty-year old what you can see through the eyes of a twenty-year old..."* and, there's *nothing* like looking through the eyes of an eighty-three-year old, especially if cataracts haven't clouded your vision!

Though I would never have admitted it back in 1944, a few years later, I came to grips with the reality that I did not like change. I preferred the constancy of life; the continuity of a set routine, knowing what had to be done and doing it, then resting in the satisfaction of accomplishment.

Agnes, however, was the complete opposite. She ventured into things with the expectation of learning something new--which she always did. I'm not suggesting that she would have joined the WAACs--certainly not--because, as she had said so many times throughout our lives, she was a *realist* and the reality was that she resisted routine at every opportunity and viewed anything "routine" as boring, unimaginative, and being on a treadmill of mediocrity.

She loved a challenge and wasted no time giving up a pursuit if reality--for whatever reason--dictated otherwise. I somehow failed to understand that part of her as we were growing up. Failure was not part of her vocabulary anymore than failing to try was part of her psychological character.

My job continued at the Englewood Theater which was very pleasant and a stress-free environment, quite the contrary to my previous work.

December 22 was my day off from work. Sam called later that day to say it was necessary for him to go to Newark to pick-up a clock part for a repair his father was doing. He invited me to go along with him. I remember it was a real wintry day, and it was snowing.

At about six that evening, we were hurrying along the snow-covered sidewalk on Broad Street to the store where he would get the clock part. Sam stepped up to the window of Jordan's Jewelers and said, "Come on, I want to go inside for a minute."

He liked watches and clocks and walked up to the clerk standing at the case displaying ladies rings and asked the man to take a few rings from the black velvet-lined trays.

"Mouse..." (That was the nickname he always called me!) "See which one of these fits you the best."

"For what reason?"

"Just try them on, *please*. I want to give you a Christmas present."

I thought: *this isn't what I expected.* They were truly beautiful diamond rings.

"Does that one fit? Do you like it?"

When I nodded, he removed his wallet and proceeded to pay the clerk the cash for the ring. (Remember, credit cards were not used sixty years ago, and Sam had no intention of paying for it on time.) So, out of the store I walked with a diamond ring on my finger. "Exactly what does this mean?"

Sam took my elbow and temporarily halted my stepping into the falling snow. "For most people it means they're engaged. Of course, we're just like *most people*, so, now consider us engaged."

First the WAACs, now I'm engaged. They'll surely think I'm crazy!

We had celebrated with dinner at a Chinese restaurant and went to a movie, which I believe was "*Here Come the Waves,*" then caught a bus to Hackensack, then another to West Englewood. (The reason we traveled by bus was to conserve the need for gasoline should Sam or his father get a call to repair a lock, in which case they would use their car.)

Have Yourself a Merry Little Christmas played that holiday season, along with Phil Brito's *You Belong to My Heart,* and *You're Nobody Til Somebody Loves You.*

I was twenty-two, Sam was twenty-four and as the year's spent months gave way to 1945, I began to sense that my comfortable cocoon of continuity was tenuous, at best.

The world was mourning the death of the Big Band leader, Glenn Miller, whose airplane was reported lost somewhere over the English Channel as he headed to Paris for a special broadcast performance for our victorious troops.

1945

The Federal Debt was reported to have risen to $260.1-Billion, with Federal Spending reported at $92.71-Billion. Unemployment remained around 1.9% because we were *still* at War.

Rum and Coca-Cola was the Andrews Sisters' hit that year, following their *The Boogie, Woogie, Bugle-Boy of Company B* four years earlier. Frank Sinatra and Gene Kelly were standing tall for all the swabees in their current film hit, *Anchors Aweigh. The Bells of St. Mary's* gave us a chaste Ingrid Bergman and the lovable character actor, Barry Fitzgerald.

The success of the D-Day invasion (though costly) and the Allies' advances raptured the American people with a renewed spirit that we were nearing the end of the war.

The Soviet offensive against Hitler's Nazi divisions in Eastern Europe, found the dead and dying in Auschwitz and Birkenau concentration camps in Poland.

Stateside, Private Eddie Slovik was the first American soldier to be executed for desertion in wartime. (The soldier who threw grenades into a tent killing and maiming his comrades in Iraq--or the soldier who feigned being kidnapped in Iraq--somehow didn't qualify on the same disgrace scale, while the soldiers babysitting captured terrorists in Abu Ghraib did. It appears that one is now guilty of the grave offense for *humiliating* terrorist prisoners who, if given the chance, would cut off the heads of every American--soldier or not!)

The start of 1945 carried a glow of expectation for the new little member of the family who was due to arrive in mid-May, the doctor's calculation for the arrival of Agnes' baby. She couldn't have been happier because May in New Jersey is quite beautiful with the multitudes of blossoming flowers and vibrant hues of green in the various trees.

Our spirits were lifted in an amazing way. I even took to looking at baby clothes and thought, *What in the world does a little baby want,* without realizing what the little tike would *need.* I found myself detouring in the stores to the baby department to browse the shelves and racks of tiny clothes, blanket, bibs, and such.

And, *I Can't Begin To Tell You* (as Bing Crosby sang to Betty Grable in the *Dolly Sisters)* that our Mother was (im)patiently waiting and counting the days until she would become a *Grandma.* In a sense, I think the four of us never forgot how it was to have in our midst the joy of a little person, such as our baby brother, who had passed away only twelve years earlier.

January was uneventful; I went to work, and the war continued. We wallpapered Agnes' room in preparation for the baby and shopped for a crib. Baby carriages were priced, because we had to plan for its purchase with the continuing ration restrictions.

Mom spent more time with Agnes while my time was consumed at the theater. It was a very special time for our Mother whose eyes showed joy and whose voice carried a happiness we had not heard in a long time. We even noticed how she tapped her toe each time she heard Les Brown's *My Dreams Are Getting Better All The Time.*

My Mother called me at the theater one day in March, and asked me to come home right away. Sam's brother-in-law had phoned to say that Sam was in the hospital in critical condition. Mom asked if there had been an accident. "No," he said. "Sam has a heart problem, but the doctors haven't yet completed their diagnosis. All things considered, please get the message to Margaret and, hopefully, she can come here as soon as possible." He said that one of Sam's relatives would meet me at the 168th Street bus terminal.

A little after five o'clock that evening, I took the bus to the terminal where one of Sam's relatives said they would meet me. He and his father had ben visiting his sister in Brooklyn, near Coney Island Avenue. Cumberland Hospital, where Sam was admitted, was not far from the Brooklyn Navy Yards that were built in the early 1800s. The hospital was known to have some very competent physicians though doctors were in short supply.

One of Sam's sisters met me and said that Sam had been diagnosed with *Bacterial Endocarditis.* The doctors detected a damaged heart valve which, they assumed, Sam had as a result of Rheumatic Fever when he was a little boy. The doctors explained that

Sam was receiving an "experimental" treatment of heavy doses of penicillin and was under strict observation. They admitted that scientists were still discovering the many uses of penicillin. (The protocols that governed Sam's treatment were, subsequently, written up in several medical journals.)

I couldn't believe what I was hearing. Sam had been in the best of health and spirits all the years I knew him. Now, he lay in a hospital bed only twenty-four-years old with an undetermined prognosis for his recovery. I was stunned, unable to justify the unfairness that had befallen him.

My world had been turned upside-down as I made three and four trips each week into Brooklyn to see Sam. He seemed to rally with each visit which gave me hope that the time I spent at his side made a difference to him. To have done less would have been unconscionable.

The newspapers were filled with reports about Roosevelt's trip to Yalta where he met Churchill and Stalin who were all as *Close As Pages in a Book*. We read of how Douglas MacArthur, finally, was permitted to fulfill his promise to return to the Philippine Islands while the city of Dresden was pummeled by American and British bombs.

The Country rallied when the photo of our Marines hoisting the American Flag at the top of Mount Surabachi on Iwo Jima reached our magazines and newspapers. *Day By Day* our hearts lifted when word came that American planes had bombed Tokyo. Maybe the world would soon be at peace.

April punctuated the final months of the War in very profound ways: American troops landed in Okinawa which, as history has recorded, turned out to be the last Pacific campaign of the War. Allied troops freed the near dead at the Nazi's Bugenwald concentration camp.

It was a Thursday, April 12, 1945 that brought the news of Franklin Delano Roosevelt's death while vacationing in Warm Springs, Georgia. And how well I remember that day...

It was slightly cloudy and unusually cool by four-thirty that afternoon when I stepped off the subway at the Dekalb Avenue Station. I walked to the change booth to pay my ten cents for the trolley ride to Cumberland Hospital. The woman was crying as I approached her; she said, "Our president is dead." I thought she meant that the president of the trolley line had died and I politely said, "I'm sorry to hear that."

"President *Roosevelt* is dead," she said. When I reached the street level, I heard the news boys hawking their papers, shouting the front page headline: "PRESIDENT ROOSEVELT DEAD!"

Vice President, Harry Truman, took the Presidential Oath of Office as Germany was being cut in two by American and Soviet forces at the Elbe River, and Bing Crosby sang, *It's Been a Long, Long Time*.

Our Mother reserved her comments when American newspapers ran the photo of Benito Mussolini, along with his mistress, who were hanging upside down from poles in a town square in Italy. (If only he had heeded his visit with the Pope!)

On the last Sunday morning in April, Agnes complained about not feeling right. Our Mother restricted her activity. At about nine o'clock that evening, Agnes began to have severe pains.

"Sometimes the baby can arrive ahead of schedule," Mom said, as Dad left for his eleven p.m. to seven a.m. shift. We called Doctor Jordan who suggested that we get Agnes to the hospital immediately.

I asked Mom to notify Peter (who was now stationed in Norfolk, Virginia) while I called a cab to take Agnes to Holy Name Hospital on Teaneck Road. In those days, the hospital maternity unit restricted all visitors (as did the Nuns who were especially strict), and only one visitor was allowed in a patient's room.

At approximately nine o'clock in the morning on April 30, at about the time Hitler and Eva Braun were committing suicide in Berlin, Agnes delivered her baby girl. I was officially an aunt. I called Mom with the good news and she confirmed that Peter was "on his way," having to take a ferry boat from Norfolk to Cape May in New Jersey where he caught a train to Grand Central in New York City, a subway to the George Washington Bridge, then a bus to Englewood. He was given a two-week shore leave. I waited with Agnes until Mom arrived and then left for home to freshen up before I went to see Sam in Cumberland Hospital. That last week in April had me curtailing my trips to visit with Sam.

I walked down Manhattan Avenue and through the low-hanging haze that early Spring morning, I met Peter walking up Manhattan Avenue to catch the #72 bus that would take him to the hospital.

Later that day, as I opened the door to Sam's hospital room, he looked up with a big smile, eager to hear of the birth of his niece? or nephew? Sam was in high spirits. "Well, what do we have," he asked with excitement in his voice.

"A little niece, named Diane. Agnes loved the song from *Seventh Heaven*," I said. The nurse congratulated me as I shared the excitement of my Mother's joy who, also, was in *seventh heaven!*

In May, events were moving at a fevered pitch: the Soviets officially occupied Berlin, while General George Patton was delayed in the field. More and more concentration camps were being discovered--along with hundreds of thousands of bodies at Neuengamme in Hamburg, and Mauthausen. May 7th marked Nazi Germany's official and unconditional surrendered.

Business came to a screeching halt with the announcement on Tuesday, May 8th, the official declaration of the Allies' Victory in Europe (V-E Day). The Country's People, and those in Englewood, too, began filling the streets. Women were singing, and most everyone appeared emotionally spent as tears of joy, and those of sadness for loved ones who would never come home, streamed down faces . Six years of the Peoples' prayers for an end to the death and destruction in

Europe had been answered; the Almighty was still listening to the world's prayers for those fighting in the Pacific.

The doctors at Cumberland Hospital told me their prognosis for Sam: the penicillin treatment had arrested the bacteria that invaded his heart; it did not--and could not--correct Sam's enlarged heart or the damaged heart valve. Sam was given only ten years to live.

I walked down the long halls of the hospital wing toward his room, thinking of what the doctors had said: "It's not for us to tell you what you should do about your upcoming marriage, Miss Griffin."

No. It certainly isn't their decision.

"He might survive the ten years, he might not. And his condition will most certainly worsen as he grows older."

Everyone worsens as age consumes the body.

I opened the door to Sam's room. He was sitting in the chair next to the window, a broad smile lighting his face. He looked straight into my eyes. "I'm not dead yet--and, I don't plan to be, regardless of what the doctors say!" And Vaughn Monroe's *Til The End of Time* weighed heavy on my mind.

Within days, Sam was released and stayed on with his sister in Brooklyn for further recuperation. When he felt strong enough, he came for dinner and then we went to a movie. His eyes danced as he lifted my new little niece up into his arms. "She's a feisty one!" he said, hugging the baby.

He acted as though the last three months hadn't happened, or that the physicians' "death sentence" had never been pronounced. That was Sam. Spirited, proud, and fiercely independent. I suppose that's what really attracted me to him. I was terribly independent, and knew it. I also knew that regardless of how much time the Good Lord was going to give Sam, I had to give him time to get back on his feet to reclaim his total independence.

As we approached the monument in Englewood, I stopped and slipped the ring off of my finger, and held it out to him.

He stared at the ring. "You're walking away?"

"No, Sam. You need money right now."

"We're engaged. You gave me your word."

"I did give you my word. I'm not breaking my promise because of your heart condition," I said. "You need to put some money away until you can get back to work."

"I've told everyone we're getting married. So, we're getting married!"

I nodded confirmation, knowing that he understood what I was saying and that it was the right course of action. I had thought it through and decided I was ready for marriage. The years we had spent dating had confirmed that I did enjoy being with him and I loved his self-confidence and manliness. Though I was extremely concerned about his health, I knew we could have a good life together. I believed that if Sam only had ten years to live, we would have a good life together for as long as God would allow.

Rogers' and Hammerstein's *June is Bustin' Out All Over*, from their Broadway hit, *Carousel,* might have motivated Harry Truman to deliver his ultimatum to Japan for an unconditional surrender, though it was ignored.

Before the end of July, a rather bizarre accident occurred: an Army airplane crashed into the Empire State Building, killing a dozen people, though the damage was nothing compared to the September 11, 2001 terrorist attacks on the Twin Towers at the World Trade Center.

It took *"Little Boy"* and *"Fat Man"* to force Japan to capitulate...

On August 6, 1945, the U.S. dropped *Little Boy,* an atomic bomb, on Hiroshima. Everyone was shocked at the catastrophic death and destruction.

Two days later, the Soviet Union "declared war" on Japan(!) "High time," our Dad said, "I wonder if they'll be wanting us to give them that bomb for their arsenals, as well."

On August 9, the U.S. dropped *Fat Man,* the second atomic bomb, on Nagasaki, Japan. Agnes and Peter celebrated their first anniversary, August 14. Of all their happy fifty-eight years of celebrating, I always remembered 1945's. Peter had survived the war and was celebrating his being a Dad.

On Wednesday, August 15, Japan surrendered. V-J Day (Victory-Japan) brought another huge celebration to Times Square and in hometowns across America.

The War was over!

History has recorded that on that same August 15, Korea split into North and South Korea, setting the stage--unbeknownst to the People--for the Korean War five short years later.

On Sunday, August 19, Ho Chi Minh took control of Hanoi in Vietnam, setting the stage for twenty years later, when our boys would be sent off to yet another war--though, unfortunately, an "undeclared" war. (I have always believed that it was our Nation's greatest disgrace when our young boys, men and women came home from *that* war, that they were neither respected for their sacrifices, nor given a *Thank You* for the hell they endured as the pawns on LBJ's chessboard.)

On Sunday, September 2, General Douglas MacArthur and Admiral Chester Nimitz accepted Japan's official surrender. The propagandist *Tokyo Rose* was arrested in Japan as American forces occupied South Korea, while the Soviets occupied North Korea. To all intents and purposes, all of the Lend-lease war materiel we sent to the Soviet Union meant nothing to them as we silently marched into the *Cold War.* The forty-four year *Cold War* allowed the people of Eastern Europe to be the slaves of the Soviet Union. Or, was that one of FDR's "concessions" to "Uncle Joe" Stalin for taking all of our money, food and war materiel?

Woodrow Wilson's failed League of Nations was replaced with the United Nations, which, I don't believe, has given any profound justification for existing unless, of course, we jump forward sixty years as some in that august body try to hide the thievery of the "Oil for Food" scandal that barely reverberates those "hallowed" walls.

The World Bank was created, and the American People wondered exactly *who* was going to provide the world's money. Ingrid Bergman and Gregory Peck starred in Alfred Hitchcock's *Spellbound,* which appropriately summed up how we all felt as America's fighting men started coming home...

In October of 2000, my son, Ronald, and I traveled back to West Englewood to see the old home place. The 120-year-old *cottage* had changed so much. I stood in the front yard, looking to where our little garden once overflowed with the vegetables we had planted and worked so hard to nurture during the Depression.

I walked along that narrow path beside the house and saw...

...my little sister playing with our brother as Mom planted that tiny maple tree while Dad made us a tree swing...

...little Agnes, dressed in a friend's grown-up clothes, pushing her dolls in that decorated box singing, *The Object of My Affection...*

...the two of us standing over the smoldering remains of our first Holy Communion veils and our Mother saying: *"Nothing is forever, and only faith will get us through the worst of this..."*

...Sam and I deciding on a day-long visit to Manhattan and Battery Park...

...the snow falling when I stood with Agnes as she cried for all the young men at war...

...that hot August day as Agnes and Peter posed for wedding photos before departing for their honeymoon...

I walked that narrow path, my footprints stepping on memories alive and living, and it was yesterday again. There are those who say, *you can never go back in time*. How sad it is they fail to realize that all of our today's and how we live them *are* tomorrow's memories...

Thoughts of Passing Time

Agnes Griffin-D'Alema(c)

The blue of an ocean, the blue of a sky,
The warmth of a smile from some passerby...
The laughter of children as they play in the park,
The tears of sadness from a broken heart...
Did I stay and help that day--
That friend in need as I passed his way?
Did I do all that I could have done--
Or, did I always just cut and run?

The heart grows heavy as one grows old...
I thought that riches were only gold.
Now days grow shorter, the memories dim...
The sight is not what it once had been.
Still, the mind has gathered so many things...
The mind has gathered so many things.
Why had these things not mattered
So long ago?

Tell us what you think about Marge Glausier's book:

1. I bought the book because:
   - ❒ the cover intrigued me
   - ❒ I heard Marge Glausier on a radio/tv talk show
   - ❒ I like reading about the past
2. I think Marge Glausier's writing is:
   - ❒ unique and different
   - ❒ powerful--I couldn't put the book down
   - ❒ sensitive and compelling
3. The book made me:
   - ❒ understand so much about the past that I never realized
   - ❒ think of how
4. The book should:
   - ❒ never have been written
   - ❒ be read by adults and youth alike to understand our past
   - ❒ be made into a movie!
5. I want to know:
   - ❒ when Marge Glausier next book is coming out
   - ❒ when Marge Glausier will be talking about her book on TV
   - ❒ when the book will be available on audiocassette or CD
6. I will:
   - ❒ tell my friends to buy this book
   - ❒ ask my library to order Marge Glausier's book
   - ❒ ask my local radio/tv talk show to interview Marge Glausier

NAME____

ADDRESS______________________________________

CITY____________________STATE____ZIP__________

EMAIL____

❒ Please put my name on FirstWorks' mailing list

❒ Send me an autographed copy of *Stepping On Memories* ($23.95) (Plus GA 6% sales tax and $4.50 S/H)

❒ Check is enclosed (*please allow 3-4 weeks for delivery)*

❒ Money Order is enclosed (*shipped within 48 hours*)

Make Check/M.O. Payable to:

FirstWorks Publishing Co., Inc.
PO Box 93 / Marietta, GA 30061-0093

FirstWorks Upcoming Titles

LOST IN YESTERDAY
by Peter Bonner

WHORE OF MADNESS
by Dani Dubre'

Titles Currently Available:

THE PALE HORSE COMETH
by Dani Dubre' & Rod Mauck

SUGAR IN THE GOURD
by Ben Garrison

INTO THE TWILIGHT
by S.W.Lowery

Printed in the United States
39269LVS00004B/16-75

9 780971 615847